AFTERSHOCKS

HEALING PTSD
FROM SEXUAL ASSAULT *and*
CHILDHOOD SEXUAL ABUSE

SUSAN BRUNSON, LCSW

To order additional copies of this book, contact:
Bookwhip
1-855-339-3589
https://www.bookwhip.com

TABLE OF CONTENTS

We have this Treasure (His Light in us)
in jars of clay to show that this All Surpassing
Power is from God, and not from us. 2 Corinthians 4:7

PREFACE

M Y INTENTION IN writing this book is to teach what I have learned and continue to learn about the miracle of healing that God gives to His children through their redemption in Christ—with emphasis on healing from the devastating and multilayered damage from sexual assault and childhood sexual abuse. This miracle healing includes healing into wholeness. I want to share information about life-changing therapies that are now available to assist and guide in healing processes. As a survivor of early childhood sexual abuse myself, I have suffered many of the issues discussed in this book. I have also had amazing healing from cutting edge therapies, wonderful therapists, and through my Christian spirituality.

It is estimated that 20 million out of 112 million women, 18 % in the USA, have been sexually assaulted/raped during their lifetime. Only 16 % of all rapes are reported to law enforcement.

Estimates of the number of adults who were sexually abused as children in the USA are one-third of all females and one-sixth to one-fourth of all males. With the 2010 USA census showing a population of over 310,000,000 people—that makes more than 24 million females and 12-19 million males who are adults now and were victims of childhood sexual abuse. That's about ¼ of the adult population. We also know that inherent in sexual abuse and physical abuse—is emotional abuse and neglect.

If you were sexually assaulted as an adult or abused as a child, or know someone intimately who was abused, then you have some awareness of the extent of the damage caused by this evil behavior enacted by one human being upon another. In childhood sexual abuse, the harm is immediate. And it is tragic because it shatters a child's innocence and personal boundaries of respect and safety. The harm we will talk about covers life long effects as well, which the child usually tries to cope with alone due to the secrecy and shame involved in abuse.

WARNING

Many readers who were sexually assaulted, sexually abused as children, or witnessed the abuse of others, will possibly be triggered as they read the stories of abuse and recovery in this book. This means you may have traumatic memories and sensations, nightmares, and intense emotions at times that are stirred up. It is best if you have someone trustworthy that you can talk with about these feelings as they arise. Even better, is to be in therapy, having your own therapist to assist you in dealing with your reactions. You can also benefit from writing your feelings in a journal, which can help in your healing process.

The current research on psychological healing from trauma and Post Traumatic Stress Disorder (PTSD) is a guide to the emotional undercurrents that we need to understand about the wounds of rape and childhood sexual abuse, and the necessity for healing. We are now blessed with several cutting edge therapies that gently and rapidly facilitate healing in patients. These therapies are grouped under the heading of Energy Psychology techniques. However, these therapies are not yet mainstream and most patients, physicians, and even therapists are unfamiliar with them. These newer "thinking outside of the box" therapies empower us with 21st century technology and tools, and advanced knowledge of whole-brain (right hemisphere and left hemisphere) functioning. The awesome science of Quantum Physics—the study and knowledge of how Energy works—is applied by using the energy of our thoughts, emotions, and body to help us heal. These therapies will be discussed in the next to the last chapter of this book "The New Therapies".

Most importantly, in learning the Truth of God's vast love for each of us—by sending His son, Jesus Christ, to live with us, love us, lead us and redeem us—we can discover that our Redemption includes the power to heal. For the reader who is already a follower of Christ, you will learn of all your rights to healing through your redemption. If you are not a Christian, you can discover the unmatched benefits of becoming a believer. So….fasten your seat belts as we fly into a new millennia of healing, with the miracles that transport us there, designed by our Creator!

"The Spirit of the Lord is upon me. He has sent me to give good news to the poor, to make well those who are broken hearted, to set at liberty those whose lives have been shattered, to make the wounded free from their chains." Luke 4:18

With love in Christ,

Susan Brunson, LCSW

CHAPTER 1

SEXUAL ASSAULT OF ADULTS

I DID NOT ORIGINALLY plan to write about sexual assault of adult victims, though I have worked in therapy with clients with these traumas for years. However, in the Fall of 2018, I and other therapists had an influx of adults seeking trauma therapy for sexual assault that had happened to them from ages 18 and up. Some had been traumatized years earlier and had never sought therapy. Others had recent traumas of sexual assault. It was like they now had social permission to admit they'd been assaulted and to seek help.

At the end of this chapter I'll list statistics from the Huffington Post in 2017 for sexual assault of adults in the USA. We might assume that adults have more resources and skills to deal with these traumas than do children and teens who are sexually abused. But—overwhelming trauma is beyond the limits and coping skills of most people, and adults feel they are rendered highly vulnerable in terrifying life or death situations and emotions. They suffer with many of the same symptoms and issues of victims of childhood sexual abuse. So some or all of the chapters included may very well hit home for adults.

Maggie was beginning to date Joe, a college acquaintance and was excited about their third date to a fraternity party. She wasn't used to drinking alcohol much and ended up drunk. She was making out with Joe upstairs in one of the bedrooms and passed out. When she came to Joe was on top of her raping her and she begged him to stop. She yelled that he was hurting her and she didn't want to have sex, but he ignored her and could care less. Later she blamed herself for being drunk and alone with him before she knew him well. She only told one girlfriend-- who told her that happens all the time and minimized the trauma. Maggie developed a deep sense of shame and decreased self-worth. She was anxious and couldn't focus in class or on her homework. She gained twenty pounds from emotional over eating and subconsciously she felt she wasn't attractive to men so she felt more safe.

Amanda took a business trip for five days to Chicago and was so excited about going to a new place. She met many interesting colleagues in her field at the huge conference. At a networking event one night she had one glass of wine and mingled with other professionals. As she walked back to her hotel room she realized she was dizzy and queasy and didn't know what was wrong. At her door she fumbled for the key card to slide and unlock her door. Suddenly a large man took the card from her, opened the door to her room, shoved her inside, and threw her on the bed. She passed out and didn't remember much when she awoke hours later, but she knew she had been attacked and raped. She called the hotel security and they called the police. When she returned home and to work she had PTSD and was constantly hyper vigilant. She felt unsafe anywhere she went. She had nightmares and flashbacks. At her mother's urging she went to get therapy from a trauma specialist.

Karen was leaving work late and it was already dark. She walked to her car in the large covered parking deck of her corporate building. She was unlocking her car when she saw a strange man moving out of the shadows rapidly and coming at her. She felt terror and a cold freezing chill. She had pepper spray on her key ring and flipped the switch to use it, spraying it directly at his eyes just as he came to within a few feet from her. She saw he had a crowbar in his hand. He immediately yelled and bent over with tears streaming out of his eyes and nose. Karen was able to get into her car, lock the doors, and screech out of the parking deck. Even though she avoided being attacked and possibly raped or killed, she developed symptoms of PTSD which took a toll on her work life and personal life. She would not work late any longer and had to walk to her car with another person. She couldn't sleep well, eat, or relax. She had catastrophic fears daily. She finally went to an EMDR therapist and got relief and healing.

The following statistics were quoted from the <u>Huffington Post</u> 2017 give us a startling view of the prevalence of sexual assault on adult victims:

90% of adult rape victims are female.

81% of women who experience rape, stalking, or physical violence by an intimate partner reported short or long term impacts such as PTSD.

94% of women experience PTSD during the two weeks directly after being raped.

13 % of female rape survivors will attempt suicide.

17,700,000—the estimated number of women who have been victims of rape since 1998.

2,780,000—the estimated number of men raped since 1998

300,000 college women were raped in 2006. Only 12 % of these rapes were reported to law enforcement.

About 35% of women who were raped as minors, also were raped as adults, compared to 14% of women without an early rape history.

28% of male rape victims were first raped when they were 10 years old or younger. Males tend to not report their victimization which may affect statistics. Some men even feel societal pressure to be proud of early sexual activity, regardless of whether it was unwanted.

Assault in the military is common. In 2014 there were at least 20,300 members of the military who were assaulted. Reporting assault in the military is low, with 85% of victims not reporting in 2014. More than 60% of military women who reported their assaults were found to have experienced retaliation. This is not surprising since 1 in 7 assaults are someone in the victim's chain of command.

EFFECTS OF SEXUAL ASSAULT:

40% of victims have work or school problems.

37% of victims have problems in the family or among friends, and inability to trust.

84 % of victims experience problems professionally and emotionally

CHAPTER 2

CHILDHOOD SEXUAL ABUSE: LAYERS AND LAYERS OF HARM

THIS CHAPTER THROWS light on the overall damage caused when an adult inflicts sexual abuse on a child or teenager, or when a teenager abuses a child. We know that at least 1/3 of female children and 1/6-1/4 of male children are sexually abused as children. Since most of the abuse is not reported, this data comes from statistics of patients who disclose the abuse in treatment, along with the data from child human resource agencies and police departments. Research also indicates that in 75% of the incidents of child sexual abuse, the abuser is someone the child knows. Most often the abuser is a family member, with most abuse being perpetrated by adult males. The fact that this atrocity is committed by a human being who is supposed to be a safe person and responsible adult in the child's life—whether a parent, grandparent, uncle, teacher, coach, priest, etc—magnifies the horror and complexity of the trauma to the child victim.

The actions of sexual abuse include any behavior, words, and intent to use a child for the perpetrator's sexual stimulation and gratification. This covers suggestive, inappropriate remarks; gazing/looking at the child lustfully; sexual touch of any part of the child's body or having the child touch the perpetrator's body sexually. It also includes forcing overt sexual acts on the child of fondling, masturbation, oral sex, intercourse, anal sex; exposing the child to pornography or to adults having sex; and any multiple-perpetrators sex acts. Any forced act of penetration in sexual abuse (whether by a penis, fingers, or other objects) feels like a form of rape to the child—physically and emotionally.

The incident of sexual abuse may occur only one time to the child and still cause significant harm and long term damage to the child's psyche. More often, the abuse occurs repeatedly, sometimes over many years of the child's life.

When the abuse first happens, the child is shocked, confused, and overwhelmed with anxiety and fear. The young child rarely knows anything about even normal, healthy sex—so they aren't sure what has happened, BUT—they know they are being harmed and are powerless. Not only is the perpetrator older and bigger; but they usually have some assumed authority over the victim by being an adult, family member, teacher, neighbor, parent's friend, babysitter, etc. Almost universally the child feels an "odd, sickening feeling in their stomach" when the sexual abuse occurs.

With progressive incidents of sexual abuse by the perpetrator, the child feels terrorized, trapped like a hunted animal, helpless, and filled with shame. They feel worthless, dirty, and damaged. Because the perpetrator often threatens the child that "If you tell anyone—I will kill your ___(ex. mother, or siblings, or pets…) and nobody will believe you anyway." And so, very few children are able to tell anyone what is happening to them. The terror, rejection, and shame is tremendous. Another extremely sad fact is that of the few children who do tell an adult (trying to seek help out of the hell they are enduring), many get rejected by family members.

The family may think that it is more shocking and damaging to consider that a relative or other "trusted" adult would ever molest a child, than to believe the child was harmed. Consequently instead of protecting the child and stopping the abuse, the adult tells the child that she is lying, or to keep "it" quiet, shaming her further. Tragically the innocent child is re-wounded now, unable to trust anyone to save her, and feels "thrown to the wolves". In fact, I have come to see those healthy family members who respond to the child's testimony with support and rescue, as heroic individuals, so rarely does it happen. Even more miraculous are the extraordinary family members who NOTICE something is wrong with the child's emotions and behaviors, then take responsibility to discover the cause of the pain they see in the child. It takes courage to stop the abuse, protect the child, and get professional help.

The age of the child at the time the molestation begins is significant in ramifications of her stage of human development. At whatever stage she is in, the initial intrusive wounding has an immediate effect on the psychological self and on the child's ability to learn and master the normal developmental tasks of that stage. Because the child's energy now must be diverted to trying to endure and survive the abuse, she is usually not able to flourish. When she moves into the next required stage of development, she is already psychologically handicapped, making each successive stage more difficult. For this reason we'll look briefly at a well-known theory of the stages of childhood development to understand the potentially damaging impact of abuse at each stage.

Eric Erickson, was a Danish-German-American developmental psychologist and psychoanalyst known for his theory on social development of human beings. He is considered as one of the originators of Ego Psychology, and was an outstanding clinician and professor, teaching at Harvard and Yale. His most famous book, "Childhood and Society", (1950) is noted for his research on the development of identity through stages of development.

Stages of Psychosocial Development

Stage 1	Age
Infancy:	Birth–18 months
Strength:	Drive & Hope
Developmental Task:	Trust vs. Mistrust

The infant's basic needs must be met including a nurturing significant caretaker, such as the mother, with visual contact and nurturing touch. In Stage 1 when the infant is sexually abused—and yes, it does happen—the baby is wounded severely in the ability to Trust. While all children who have been abused have great struggles with trying to figure out WHO they can be SAFE with (not sexually abused, used, harassed, or demeaned by), the baby of course is most vulnerable and fragile. Being unable to Trust his environment, and possibly one of his primary caretakers, the baby has difficulty generating motivational Drive and Hopefulness, which are the Strengths to be acquired in this developmental stage.

Jamie began to notice that her baby, Amy, was having restless nights with less sleep, crying, and sometimes screaming out, as if in fear. Jamie moved the baby's crib into the master bedroom to keep watch. This helped for a few nights, then Amy continued with her sleeplessness.

Jamie took the baby to her pediatrician, Dr. Smith, who gently examined her and asked the mother a series of questions about physical signs and symptoms. Finally he began to ask about people in Amy's life.

"Have there been any disturbing events or any new people coming around the baby?"

Jamie pondered and thought- "Yes, we have a new babysitter who's been coming for the past two months."

Dr. Smith asked "Did Amy show these sleep problems before the new baby sitter came?"

Jamie frowned, "No, I don't think so."

"Well, I'd consider not using that baby sitter any more. She may be doing something that is frightening the baby," recommended Dr. Smith.

Jamie decided to not call the babysitter again. A few weeks after the babysitter no longer came to the house, Amy's sleep returned to normal.

Studies in infant brain capacity in the past decade have shown that babies have the ability to remember images and feeling sensations as young as 6 months old. Sometimes after she has been abused, or exposed to some other traumatic event as an infant, the child will remember the trauma in images and sensations. Later, when she gains language, she may speak of the events.

Stage 2	Age
Early Childhood:	18 months–3 years
Strength:	Will
Developmental Task:	Autonomy vs. Shame & Doubt

The most significant relationship now is with both the parents. The child's self-esteem is developing. In Stage 2 with the toddler of 18 months to 3 years of age, the child's budding sense of autonomy (wanting to have some separation from his parents through learning to talk, walk, and explore), is shaken by the trauma of his sexual abuse. The emerging self-esteem is crushed—leaving the toddler with intense feelings of Shame and Self-Doubt. The Strength of this stage "Will" is distorted now. The child may behave passively, not exerting his will in healthy ways, or may identify himself as "bad" and become destructive.

It seemed to Toby's parents that he had mysteriously read books about the "Terrible Two's" because he showed every difficult behavior of that phase. When his temper tantrums became more frequent and he was breaking toys and hitting other children, his parents felt worried, frustrated, and helpless to make him behave. They tried time-outs and rewards with only small effect. Finally by the time Toby was 4 his aggressive behavior and agitation had decreased.

Years later Toby revealed to his older brother that when he was very young, probably 2–3 years old, one of his brother's friends had molested him several times. The boy had told Toby "Don't tell anyone or I will beat you up". So, he didn't. He wouldn't have known how to say what was happening anyway.

Stage 3	Age
Play Age:	3 years–5 years
Strength:	Purpose
Developmental Task:	Initiative vs. Guilt

Family relationships now are the most important part of the child's life. This includes parents, siblings, pets, and extended family. In Stage

3 of the child's development, when sexual abuse occurs, the 3 year old to 5 year old is harmed in the psychological area of being afraid to take the Initiative which inhibits her finding a sense of Purpose. The child feels tremendously guilty for being abused, as if it were somehow her fault, and that she should have made the abuse stop.

Laura called the community mental health center early Monday morning and exclaimed, "Last night my husband molested my 5 year old daughter—his step-daughter! I found out and confronted him. We need help!" She was seen that day for crisis intervention counseling.

Laura was a homemaker with 4 children, two from a first marriage and two from her current marriage to Stan. She told the counselor that she saw an "odd behavior" when her daughter Melody was sitting with her step-Dad, Stan in the living room in the dark watching TV. She called Melody out to the kitchen and quietly asked her if Stan had "hurt her or bothered her". Melody burst into tears and nodded yes. Laura gently asked Melody to go to her room. Then she called Stan into the kitchen. When she confronted him about touching her child in a sexual way, he denied it but grabbed his keys and left in his car.

The counselor told Laura that by law, she had to call the Department of Human Resources (DHR) to report suspected child abuse. She also asked if Stan would come in for counseling, and said that he could be required to come based on DHR's investigation. Laura said she wanted to bring Melody in for counseling and get help for all of them.

After several sessions of individual counseling with Laura, Melody, and Stan, the counselor and DHR social worker agreed that Stan had made significant progress in expressing remorse and taking responsibility for his actions, and changing. He now clearly understood his actions were very harmful to Melody, to the whole family, and are a crime with legal consequences. A family therapy session was conducted then where Laura lovingly and firmly expressed to Melody that she would always protect her and that the child could come and tell her anything. Stan genuinely apologized to Melody for his molesting her and took all the blame. He said he would never do that again, and that he could go to jail if he did. He told her he loved her and wanted to be a good step-father to her. Melody showed great relief, and got up from her chair to sit in between Laura and Stan on the couch in the counseling office.

Stage 4	Age
School Age:	6 years–12 years
Strength:	Competence
Developmental Task:	Industry vs. Inferiority

Here the social relationships expand from the family to school, neighborhood, church, and social activities such as sports, music lessons, art lessons, etc. This stage is also called the Latency Stage of pre-puberty. (However in the current times this stage often ends at age 10 as puberty occurs much younger now than in past generations). The elementary school and middle school child who is sexually abused, while being thrust into increased social relationships and responsibilities of school, family, neighborhood, is wounded in the area of perceptions of Competency. This child feels pervasively inadequate, "not good enough", inferior to others, and believes he is unable to fulfill his roles in life.

Johnny liked to visit his neighbor down the street, Mr. Jones. They would hit golf balls in the yard, with Mr. Jones teaching him how to use the clubs and hit the ball. At 10 years old Johnny was developing his athletic skills. He loved playing baseball and football, but golf was a whole different thing.

One day, after several months of visits, Johnny went into the house as they got a snack. But this time, the man he thought was his friend, attacked him from behind, threw him on the floor, and raped him. When it was finally over, Johnny was shocked, in pain, and felt ashamed, humiliated, and betrayed. Mr. Jones told him not to tell anyone because they would think Johnny was dirty and bad...... And he never told.

Stage 5	Age
Adolescence:	12 years–18 years
Strength:	Devotion & Loyalty
Developmental Task:	Identity vs. Role Confusion

The teenager feels her most significant relationships are with her peer group. Here development begins to depend on "what WE do" rather than "what is done to us" as in prior stages. In Stage 5 the child is now a teenager from 12 years old to 18 years old. Because the child's sense of Identity is altered due to the sexual abuse (as we'll see in detail in Chapter 3) she suffers Confusion in adjusting to new social, academic, and work roles. This weakens her ability to feel a sense of Loyalty to others, ideals, and goals. With this Role Confusion, a lack of focus and intent permeates. The teen sees her self as still dependent on what others do to her or for her, rather than on what she herself is capable of doing.

When Sandy, age 14, began to develop from a child to a young lady, her Uncle Bob began to stare at her body and have a "crazy" look in his eyes. She didn't like being around him. He came to eat dinner with the family one night and Sandy ate quickly, then excused herself to go wash the dishes so she could get away from Uncle Bob and her parents. The family went to sit in the living room to watch TV and talk while Sandy was cleaning up the kitchen. Uncle Bob came into the kitchen and came up behind her and grabbed her breasts possessively as he said ""You're really grown up." Sandy was frozen and couldn't find her voice. She wiggled away from him and went to her room and locked the door. There she began shaking and crying.

Later she tried to tell her mother what happened. But her mother minimized and dismissed it, not really listening to Sandy. Sandy was crushed, and felt all alone in the world. She determined she would never be around her uncle again. If he came to her house, she would be gone to a friend's house, or pretend to be sick and lock herself in her room.

Stage 6	Age
Young Adulthood:	18 years to 35 years
Strength:	Affiliation & Love
Developmental Task:	Intimacy & Solidarity vs. Isolation

The young adult's most significant relationships are with friends, a romantic or marital partner, and work colleagues. In Stage 6, the older teen of 18—20 who is sexually abused by an older adult, is damaged in the area of being able to be Intimate emotionally and sexually. They often seek to be loved by someone who will validate them as loveable and "give" them a sense of worth. Since they feel insecure, un-loveable, and worth-less they do not feel they belong anywhere. The abuse victim will unconsciously attract and be attracted to people who will dominate and be abusive to them. Lacking in the healthy emotional foundation required to develop and maintain good interpersonal relationships where intimacy can occur, they continue to isolate themselves within relationships, and by staying outside of close relationships. Thus they feel alienated from others on a one-to-one basis, as well as on a peer group basis. These feelings negatively impact their work and career progression, peer relationships with friends and family, and romantic/ marital relationships. At the time when an older teen/younger adult is normally forging her life's purpose and seeking her life mate—the child abuse victim is fighting to keep her head above the inner turmoil.

Miranda, lovely and shy at 18, really liked one of her college professors. Dr. Jane Lake was so interested in the students and they all thought she was great. Miranda admired her intelligence, her ability to teach amazing knowledge in anthropology and sociology, and her friendliness.

At the end of one of Dr. Lake's night classes, Miranda stayed after to ask her some questions. Dr. Lake said "Follow me to my office. I'll loan a book to you on this topic." Once in the office, the professor offered Miranda a seat and a coke. As they were chatting ---- and before Miranda knew what was happening, the professor put her arms around the girl and kissed her on the mouth and neck. She told Miranda "I could be very good to you." Miranda was stupefied, embarrassed, confused, and felt horribly awkward. She didn't know what to say or do...So she just blurted out "I have to go", dashing out the door and down the hall.

From whatever Stage of Development the child is first sexually abused in, the damage and lack of mastery of the tasks of that Stage carries over into each next Stage. The rippling dysfunction leaves the child unprepared for the new tasks of the new Stage, and her ability to acquire the Strengths inherent in healthy development. In summarizing how the sexual abuse wounds fester through each subsequent stage of the child's development, we see the pattern of the layers upon layers of harm. The abuse, like a gunshot blast to the heart of the child, untreated and unhealed, perpetuates the bleeding of her soul.

Perhaps we can think of the ongoing damage and pain from the sexual abuse as emotionally similar to what physically happens to a person who is severely burned: the suffering of immediate shock and horror, pain, and the damage of the burns; then the awful suffering through the "tortuous treatments" over long periods of time, with ongoing pain and scarring. Except the victim of childhood sexual abuse has wounds and scars that are hidden beneath the surface—yet filtering through her view of self, and her now distorted view of the world; and manifesting in her behaviors and relationships.

A miracle of temporary reprieve often happens in the psychological phenomena called Repression, a Defense Mechanism. This is when a person's conscious mind pushes and hides the recall of a trauma into the caverns of the subconscious mind (out of present awareness and memory). The repressed information goes underground, usually for many years, to protect the child and allow her the best chance at surviving and growing up.

Emotionally and behaviorally the child still responds to the emotional wounds and negative beliefs engendered by the abuse, but memories and causes are locked away. Only later—as an adult—does the psyche let the data leak up to the surface of conscious awareness. The shock, bewilderment, and agony of these emerging memories appear at first to be harmful to the victim. However, the psychic purpose of recovering the truth of the experiences is to push the person into seeking recovery and healing from the abuse so she can have a much better life.

It is extremely difficult to do the healing alone, because one cannot be objective about what is happening, and needs the support and wisdom of a compassionate, trustworthy helper. We benefit highly from having a competent, caring, skillful witness to our sufferings to validate the wounds, help us understand the vulnerable child we were when the abuse occurred, hear the story and feelings we need to express, and to wisely guide us into the re-discovery of who God created us to be.

TONI'S POEM

Sugar and spice and everything nice,
You're in my bed once, you're in my bed twice.

I'm closing my eyes now, my world is the Dark;
While you brand me forever with your hideous mark.

I've frozen in silence until you are through,
The minutes are hours—the pain is not new.

The smell is disgusting, you leave in your wake;
Another one's over, this Hell I can't take.

I wanted to scream, to kick and to fight;
Instead I'm your play toy when day becomes night.

My Spirit is dying, I cringe at the thought;
You must have decided my soul you had bought.

And during the day time I'm such a good girl,
All dressed up and frilly, all ribbons and curls.

No one would notice, the bruise on my thighs,
The scream in my throat, the tears in my eyes.

If only they'd hear what I couldn't quite say;
They may take this pain and this terror away.
But how could I tell when I hadn't the words?
For the language of sex to a child is absurd.

So I played with my toys, for my toys were my friends,
My dolls were my confidants, my heart they would mend.

I knew they were magic, their power was real;
To love and to comfort, to nurture, to heal.

I had no one else, my Mommy's not here.
She's out making money, "To feed you, my dear".

The nighttime is horror, it goes on and on;
He's coming now for me, there's no where to run.

The monster is breathing, the monster is real.
He's not in my storybook, his breath I can feel.

The beer is still lingering all in his breath;
And nothing can save me, there's not even death.

I was born for this purpose, I feel in my bones.
I'm just here to please him, I feel so alone.

And when it's all over, I cry in my bed;
And pull all the covers up over my head.

And dream of the flowers….the birds and the trees;
Of the day I had power, the day I was free.

And wonder where GOD is and why HE'S not there?
I feel he's my daddy… but daddy don't care.

I never once mattered, he never once cared.
He did what he wanted, he did what he dared.

And the sounds that I made were only inside;
My blood I would wash off, the sheets I would hide.

I know my Mom found them, for how could she not?
Rolled up in my closet, all tied in a knot.

A baby had taken them, put them away.
Had gone to the bathroom to clean the decay.

And crawled back in bed, like all babies do,
Grateful to know that for now he was through.

And when I awaken, the day again here;
I cannot remember….. there's nothing to fear.

But years and years later, you came back to me.
You're here in my nightmares, "to rape me, you see".

I cannot escape, can't run from my mind.
I must face the legacy you left behind.

You painted a picture, you gave it a name.
A name that's familiar, it calls itself Pain.

That's all that you gave me, that's all that I have--
Of the monster I lived with, the monster called Dad.

And then there's my mother, you said you "Would KILL!!"
Her denial has saved you, is saving you still.

She lives in her dream land, stays locked in her mind;
Refuses to hear me, can't take what she'll find.

She gave up her baby, my blood's on her head.
She left me with Daddy-- to sleep in their bed.

One day I will show her the pain in my heart.
And hold her responsible—for she had a part.

A part of the damage that plagues my life still;
And keeps me from Heaven—my REAL FATHER'S will.

I think now I'll thank Him for keeping me sane;
For <u>you</u> as a human should take ALL the blame.

They say that HE loves me, I'm trying to <u>know</u>.
I NEED HIM—to prosper, to learn, and to grow.

HE'S calling me Home now, home in my Heart.
The healings not over, but at least it's a start.

ME

TONI'S STORY

To have lived through my childhood in itself proves that miracles do happen. My life after childhood cinches the deal.

It only stands to reason that what we live day in and day out will eventually become our adult reality. My father made sure I knew my place in this world. My mother then proceeded to keep me there long after he was gone.

My attempt at anything good came only from myself. Myself and God, that is. Faith has been my birthright and friend. Without Faith my story would have remained mine alone.

My first memory of my beginning is not easy to fathom but it is what it is. I saw my father in a white starched shirt, black dress slacks, bigger that life standing over my crib. As I peered through the bars I watched him depart, disappearing through the hall. Then as if hovering above my bed I saw "me". My terry cloth sleeper was torn, my diaper was opened still covered in my own blood. My innocence/ virginity—no longer mine.

I know nothing else of that day. This memory came to me while standing in my own child's room, looking at the dolls lying on her floor. My eyes landed on an open baby diaper. And there it was like a video in my head, although in reality the diaper was clean and white, in my mind it looked red stained with my own infant blood. The same blood that ran through my father's veins. The man who ideally would have protected as "true fathers" do. Nothing was the same to me after that memory resurfaced. And nothing ever will be. My life took on a surreal quality that precedes every memory since then.

Since that day many memories have returned, each one unfolding the truth of a little girl's nightmare. That little girl is me. And I will no longer keep quiet. To do so at this juncture in my life would in fact cost me—"me". It is part of my story, a part of me that for years remained undiscovered, but not inactive. Like a volcano it would erupt into my life unexpectedly. I would rage over something trivial, and sadness like a dark cloud shrouded my mind shrouding my mind as I fought through a depression I never understood. Tears would flow like a river over something in the present that warranted a trickle. I had unexplained lapses in judgment that cost me years of my life trying to escape the awareness of the pain. My choice of a first husband was a lack of judgment. An exact replica of my father. Different name, different face, different body ---identical inside. He was addicted to alcohol… Drowning in insecurities, feeling inadequate as a man…Beating his wife into submission. He used sheer terror as a weapon to keep his victim in check. That lapse of judgment cost me four long years of hell and almost cost me my life.

The sad thing is I only took him up on his proposal to get married in order to get away from the hell I endured at home…. and because I did love him and believed my love would "fix" him. Little did I know a new kind of hell was on the horizon. One I absolutely had no resources to handle. Again God came through. There is no other way to see it.

The beatings took all I had left to survive. There were times I literally stood on the brink of insanity. I remember it now so vividly although I've only allowed myself to revisit a few rare times. I can feel what I felt in those moments. Most people will never know that sometimes, in some situations, insanity is a choice. At least it was for me. I lay in my bed, eyes fixed on the ceiling and I wondered what would happen if I let "it" happen. Time felt slowed as if my choice demanded an answer. I could hear my husband's voice calling my name over and over, getting more filled with fear each time. And I knew I could stay in that place of "nothing" forever if that's what I wanted. I have no idea how long I stayed in that state. Only that when I chose to come back...I came back different. I remember the relief in him. He was literally petrified by what he saw that day. So was I. To this day I do not know why I chose to come back...other than God doing for me what I couldn't do for myself. And I'm glad I came back...to Life. I had the courage and determination to leave him shortly after that.

The worst memory I've had by far is the night my father woke me from sleep raping me. I tried to think of a better word for what he did, but in the end, what does that matter? I was 6 years old. I truly believe he used a pillow to muffle my screams so my brothers wouldn't wake. I couldn't see and I couldn't breathe. My claustrophobia makes perfect sense after I remembered this—the smothering feeling I've carried all my life. When this memory resurfaced I was astounded at the resourcefulness of my 6 year old self. It's impossible to fathom how a child survives that horror. Again, God has helped me.

After my father left my room, I went to the bathroom and frantically washed this "stuff" off of me. I felt like if I didn't hurry and get it off it would envelope and destroy me. I could barely see for the tears and the choking sounds in my throat were deafening to me. I remember getting water all on the floor and being so afraid I would get into trouble for making a mess. As an adult that is appalling to me. I was this "frightened little adult" trying to take care of this terrorized little girl who had no words for what had just happened to her.

You better believe I have protected my own little girls with a vengeance. After I remembered the abuse, I made it my life's work. I believe that incest and/or rape of a child should be punishable by death. Any victim who has survived it deserves to be applauded, not shamed. The people who claim that repressed memories are "false memories" are wrong. And even if one child lies and says they were abused when they weren't (usually under duress from an adult), for that one child there are millions who are not lying. To not believe a victim is like murdering their soul all over again. I mean, really....who wants sexual abuse to be true for them? "My Dad raped me". Try saying that to anyone and watch their reaction. Who would want that?

That was the worst visual memory I've recovered so far. The rest are feeling memories…though I do clearly remember when toys I had then have come back in vividly detailed memories. I do know now that what we carefully block out to survive gets frozen in our minds along with the happy moments we experienced during those years. I like to think of this phenomena as the "gift within the pain". It also helps to validate the experiences. For years I was skeptical in the beginning of my recovery of abuse memories, as to whether or not this was true. Going through your life—not remembering that someone you loved and tried to understand—had in fact done these unthinkable things to you, and had gotten away with this injustice.

It is moments like that when I feel pure hatred toward my father. Forgiving him seems impossible, ANOTHER injustice to suffer. However, my hatred and rage serve nothing in retaliation.…He's already dead. He doesn't feel anything on earth any more. I can hardly voice the anguish of the child in me who feels he got off without the truth coming to light, and without punishment or retribution.

At this point I must step back and look at this differently. Two things come to mind. One is—"The secret things belong to God." Deuteronomy 29:29. Number two is "Vengeance belongs to God." Hebrews 10:30-31. So the question now is will I forgive the animal that did this to a sweet, innocent, loving, precious child? I must say "Yes" against all logic. Unforgiveness only serves to poison MY life, and does absolutely nothing to hurt my father, the perpetrator. Therefore it becomes just a little more conceivable for me to accept the unacceptable. My father *does not* deserve my forgiveness. He never did and never will. However, I do deserve to reap the benefits of once and for all, releasing this task to God.

I do believe God has special regard for those of us who endured such tragedies as children. It only makes sense. After all He is our TRUE Father. It is Him who created us. His heart swells with such a love that it moved Him to another inconceivable truth. He sent His only Son to suffer and die for us to give us Life, forgiveness, mercy, healing, and power. Jesus can understand abuse and betrayal. And He commands us to forgive so we can come full circle to the truth that sets us free. I will forgive my father. Then God will do His job. I am free.

At this point I would like to address the fellow sexual abuse survivors out there reading this book. I, like you, could not consider forgiving for a very long time. I encourage you not to give up before you get there. Forgiveness is hard…but not impossible with God's help.

My father died at 54 years old of stomach cancer. When he died I was faced with a nightmare in the making that I had no idea was coming. You see when I was the child victim he told me he would kill my mother if I told. After he died that threat was removed. In my subconscious I was then safe to remember the abuse. The memories started resurfacing almost immediately after the shock subsided from his death. I began to feel someone pushing me down on the bed at night waking me out of sleep. Nightmares flooded my sleep as I struggled to figure out what was happening to me. Then the pain hit. And boy did it hit. I remember how the thought of my father alone would cause me unbearable emotional pain… heaving, sobbing pain. I knew in my heart it was not grief from losing him. It was different than that. It was about me.

The connection became clear as I sought professional help. My world seemed to change so drastically that I didn't have anything to hold on to. If this thing was true, then everything else about my childhood was a lie. I trusted nothing in my prior perception of reality. It was absolutely the most unstable time in my entire life.

I also had buried my second husband a year before my father died. He had died in a car accident. Looking back I see his death as a portal of sorts into the issues with my father. They seemed a lot alike. I had picked a man who even looked like my father. Thank God I was referred to a wonderful woman to counsel me and the journey had begun.

My reality now is totally different as a result of facing the pain of child abuse. I'm happy to say I've managed to raise 3 wonderful children and have come to a rather pleasant phase of adulthood. I am 50 years old and happy to be so. I have a firm and secure belief in the God who loves me unconditionally. I have my children and an extra bonus of answered prayer with 5 beautiful grandchildren. I know now I'm NOT crazy (a fear I've had since childhood) and with that knowledge comes freedom.

I remember at one point in my recovery from the drug addiction (that had ensued shortly after adolescence)—as I looked through the bars in a mental institution. I was suicidal (understandably) after memories began pressing through my awareness. Funny thing is I went in to inpatient treatment suicidal, and within the first 24 hours I had become terrified someone else would actually kill me. I slept, ate, and prayed for 3 whole days in the same clothes I was admitted in. I begged the Lord to keep me safe from harm or even scarier, death, until I could get out of there. I did get out having read almost the entire Alcoholics Anonymous Big Book, to get a grasp on this thing I now knew I wanted...to be alive... to have a fighting chance...to be a good mother....to get well. I've since been free from the experience of being admitted to an institution. I intend to keep it that way. Besides, my father belonged there, I didn't.

I can also tell you the irony of that still amuses me, as awful as the actual experience was. I went in wanting to kill myself. I soon decided I didn't want to die, but there was a frightening possibility I would, if God didn't protect me. The sad reality is that many patients in institutional treatment are also repressing abuse memories, but have no clue that is the core cause of their depression, anxiety, or substance abuse problems.

If my story can help one person ...or countless victims, it will be a blessing. I am finally willing to tell my story...to help myself and others. It is high time we were free. All of us. The secrecy of childhood sexual abuse has claimed far too many of us. The damage it causes is all encompassing to the child who had no choice, no voice, and no way out. The indecent, violating, intrusive, uncaring acts of such sick people must be spoken and dealt with. It's the secrecy and denial of people who do know, but who won't help the child, that keeps the sick perpetrator protected. There is no protection for the child. Only God can do the impossible. That is why the child represses (temporarily forgets) about the abuse for years. If it were not for this protective mystery from God, I would not now be alive. The same is true for other victims of child abuse. God must have wanted us to live to tell, besides the fact that He loves us and wants us well.

I did not want this abuse. I didn't ask for it. Looking back I can see now how I became promiscuous as a young woman. That was the only way I knew how to relate to men, to get attention, and to seek to be loved. But, I stayed away from men until I married at age 17, a virgin I thought. When I remembered the rape by my father, that was the first thing I grieved. That I was not actually a virgin at marriage. Now when I tell someone how important it was to me to be a virgin, I reclaim my innocence for myself. Sex was not my choice as a child. I will not allow my father to take that from me. And, I reclaim my dignity as a human being.

I'm now in the process of learning who God, my real Father, truly is and the truth of His holiness, purity, and love. To give up now is inconceivable to me. I have a new Father now, and He would never hurt me. This leads me to the freedom I must claim and take possession of. The journey continues.....

CHAPTER 3

IDENTITY DISORDERS

"The Child is father of the man." Wordsworth.

OUR IDENTITY IS the sum of our perceptions and beliefs of WHO we ARE and what we can DO in our lives. From birth through 7 years old, children form their core beliefs about their identity, which along with their natural temperament, shapes their personality. This Identity is the foundation from which the child proceeds to function in the world. The core beliefs that children perceive, interpret, and download about their self and the world, whether people realize it or not, continue to significantly influence them as adults.

Certainly when a child is sexually abused there is a major negative impact on their sense of identity and their internal "map of the world". Being essentially vulnerable and powerless to protect themselves from a perpetrator, and being naïve about what sexual behavior is, the young child suffers through and survives this evil intrusion on their body and soul in several ways. One defense they use is <u>Dissociation</u>—using their imagination to "go somewhere else" away from their awareness of the abuse that is occurring. The child may stare at the ceiling, a door knob, or just close their eyes and pretend they are floating outside elsewhere, or are in a private hiding place. This assists them in psychologically separating from the sickening event and numbing their emotions to the abuse. This pattern of Dissociation continues outside of the abuse situation with the child staring off into space and often not remembering ordinary daily happenings. While this is adaptive and a blessing to the child survivor, this habitual behavior continuing into adulthood keeps the survivor from being fully present in awareness in the Here and Now at times. In order to experience the full joy, spirituality, and sensuality in life we need to be able to be aware in the present moment. Thus the pattern of Dissociation becomes maladaptive, interfering with the person's ability to focus, think consciously, feel their emotions and understand what they feel, and to live life fully. The instinctive response of Dissociation to the trauma can be one of the fall-out damages that keeps the victim/survivor from later enjoying healthy sexual desire and responsiveness in a loving relationship with their mate.

Claire couldn't stand the smell of dirty clothes and socks. It made her feel not only disgust, but nausea. When her mother tried to teach her how to do laundry at age 12 she felt repulsed by the smell and ran out of the basement laundry room crying. Her mother was irritated and worried. She tried to talk to Claire about her phobia but neither of them could understand or fix the problem.

Finally Claire's mother took her to a counselor who specialized in helping people with anxiety issues, and had a knack for working with kids. When the counselor was using a therapy technique called EMDR, Claire suddenly had a memory of being in the basement laundry room at her aunt's house in another state. She recalled piles of dirty, smelly clothes and then her uncle forcing her to perform oral sex on him. The therapist used the EMDR to help Claire desensitize her memory and energy system from the terrifying memory. After two sessions the experience of the abuse faded and Claire's phobia disappeared.

Children from infancy to age 12 frequently use Repression— forgetting the memory of the trauma in order to survive it. In counseling when the initial life history is taken, some people cannot remember much at all of their lives before age 10 or 12. This is a red flag that there were likely traumatic events of some kind in those early years. Brain research on infants in the past 15 years indicates that at as young as 6 months old infants can record images, sounds, and tactile sensations in their memory, which they can later access and speak about.

The child victim develops Core Negative Beliefs in forming their identity that are destructive lies—the opposite of what God wants each child to believe...."I am helpless and powerless. I am alone and unloved. I am damaged goods, worthless. I am a failure. I'll never be safe. There is no one I can trust. God has abandoned me." The Enemy, the Father of Lies, wants the child to believe these words of despair.

These inner negative beliefs form a shaky foundation for the child, who experiences massive insecurity. Pervasive feelings that "something is wrong with me" and "something bad is going to happen" prevent the child from having a sense of safety anywhere. In "Satan's Dirty Little Secret", (2007) by Steve Foss he states:

> "There are two *evil* spirits that all other *evil* spirits get their strength from: Insecurity and Inferiority. These are defined as: Insecurity—the state of being not secure, not confident, not firm. Inferiority—the state of feeling lower in position, stature, or value.....These are the doorways through which every other *evil* spirit gets its entrance.....The enemy knows that unless he can gain a stronghold in the thinking of a man, he cannot truly control that man. The enemy has no strength over us as believers except that which we give him through submitting and agreeing with his lies. The battlefield is two fold and must be fought on both fronts. It is in the heavenlies and it is in our minds."

In the book "Win Every Battle", 2009, by Michael Galiga, he states:

> "The two biggest giants that are the root causes of all our problems are Inferiority and Insecurity. Satan's gateway... to our hearts is the belief that "I'm not

enough" (Inferiority), and "If I'm not enough, I won't
be loved." (Insecurity).

Linda was a Librarian at the middle school and loved her job. In
fact, it was the only thing she loved except for her 2 cats at home in her
small apartment. She had always been a shy, quiet person. Her mother
had died when she was 11. Linda missed her companionship.

After her mother's death from a car accident, Linda and her father,
also a quiet person, led an isolated, lonely life. Her father was not an
affectionate man and although he wasn't cruel, Linda never felt close to
him. He never dated, and they never went anywhere except work and
school.

The crushing blow was when at age 15, Linda's father began to come
into her bedroom at night and molest her. He never had intercourse
with her, but he harmed her sense of safety, privacy, and decency. When
she graduated high school at age 17, she went to college far away on
scholarships and never returned home. She spoke to her father by phone
once a month in superficial politeness. She felt she could not trust men
so she never dated. Becoming a Librarian in a small town suited her
well—though she did feel very lonely at times and wondered if she'd
ever have more of a life.

The abused child rarely tells anyone of the abuse and believes they
are the only one who has ever been abused. They think other children
live in families where sexual abuse doesn't happen. They have a concept
that other families are "normal" and healthy like those portrayed on
"The Walton's" or "Leave It to Beaver". Often the child victim stays
emotionally distant from peers so no one will get to know that they are
"damaged goods".

Some abuse victims become confused about whether they are
heterosexual or gay when they are abused by someone of their same
gender. They may later act out being homosexual or bisexual to see if
that fits for them. Alternately, some victims may be so frightened by an
abuser of the opposite sex that they decide to be with a person of their
same gender to feel safe.

As abuse victims enter adolescence and young adulthood, they may vacillate between totally avoiding romantic relationships, and acting out promiscuously. They often feel the only value they have is to be used for sex. They want someone to love them but feel all they have to give is sex. Some feel the only power they have in relationships is through seducing and controlling others with sex.

The natural innocence of the child and the normal developmental passages leading to increasing knowledge and experience of intimate emotional/sexual relationships has been stolen. They have lost the opportunity to grow up learning healthy thoughts and behaviors regarding God's miraculous, beautiful, and holy gift of loving sexuality in a relationship of respect, honor, closeness, and commitment. Their perception of sex is grossly distorted into something painful, terrifying, humiliating, sickening, harmful, and manipulative. Even just one incident of sexual abuse of a child by a non-familial perpetrator (not considered as severely damaging as repeated abuse by a family member) can cause the unhealed victim to have difficulty with healthy sexual desire, intimacy, and performance in their marriage.

Tina had been married to Harvey for 20 years and loved him dearly. They had 2 children they both loved and built their lives around. Tina was a homemaker and Harvey a lawyer. Financially they did well.

Their only problems seemed to be that Harvey sometimes drank too much, and Tina rarely enjoyed their sexual relationship. She just didn't like sex. She had tried to explain that she believed the reason she never felt desire for sex with her husband, and couldn't relax during sex, had to do with the time her parents' friend, Tom, molested her when she was 8 years old.

Harvey couldn't understand how just one event could cause Tina so much hatred of sex. He felt unloved and cheated out of marital bliss. Eventually he came to believe he had a right to have great sex—so he went outside the marriage. His drinking increased due to his guilt. And the marriage began to unravel.....

Incest is the most destructive and insidious type of child sexual abuse. It is defined as sexual relations/behavior with a member of one's own biological family. With so many blended families in today's culture, we also consider incest to be abuse between step-parents and other step-relatives and a child, due to the closeness of the ties. Every culture on the planet has a strong taboo against incest. One reason is because, as we know, if a pregnancy occurs between close blood relatives, the baby has a high risk of various birth defects. Hence the tern "inbred". Besides psychological damage to a child victim of incest there is also damage to others in the family's relationship dynamics, hidden beneath the surface. When the perpetrating family member lives in the home with the child, the stress on the child is thought to be similar to that of someone living in a concentration camp. The child is constantly hypervigilant to avoid the perpetrator if possible and feels some relief only if the offender is away from the home, at work etc. The child fights going to sleep so they can be on guard if the perpetrator comes to their bedroom in the night.

In situations of incest by the father or step-father, the mother is sometimes <u>not</u> aware of the incest—since children are too frightened to tell, and the perpetrator often has threatened them. And as one mother stated, "Why would you ever think that your husband, the father of your child, would be sexual with that child?"

But in some cases mothers do have some awareness that something very wrong is happening. Rather than breaking through their own denial, observing, and questioning the child or the father, they push the suspicions into their subconscious mind with stronger denial. The thought that their mate could actually do something so unspeakable is intolerable to them. IF it is true…then the mother would HAVE to do something such as: ask their child; confront their husband; make it stop…how? What will happen to the entire family if the truth comes out? This is a psychological issue, physical abuse issue, legal issue, and marital issue. If the husband is arrested and goes to prison, what will the mother do without his income? The shame of the sexual abuse to the family, possible loss of the marriage, and the legal consequences seem too much for the mother to allow into her consciousness. (Sometimes there is even a pathological jealousy of the mother towards the child for "getting attention" sexually from the husband). These thoughts and feelings are life and death issues—so terrifying and life-threatening to the mother—who wants her family to survive. Denial is much less painful and frightening. So life goes on…..as if all were normal….*(and Satan just smiles)*.

The child begins to see that the non-offending parent is <u>not</u> going to rescue them from the abuse. So, they are all alone ---no one to trust, no one to protect them, no one to save them… No one to help them express and deal with their enormous emotional wounds. The abused child often develops "learned helplessness" in which they feel defeated, discouraged, and abandoned so often that they resign themselves to being victims and suffering. They come to believe that no effort on their own part will help them….nor do they have hope that someone else will.

Other parents are more consciously aware that sexual abuse of the child is occurring, but they "look the other way" because they are terrified and have no ability to stand up to the perpetrator and protect the child. They sacrifice the child to preserve their own survival, thinking they are doing this to help the family survive. A child who later recognizes that they have been sacrificed feels immense rage at the non-offending, non-protecting parent as well as at the perpetrating parent.

Because our core sense of identity is formed in the family unit, the child maligned by incest has a "map of the world" that is based on these severely dysfunctional and distorted experiences. Anywhere this victim of abuse goes now feels potentially unsafe ---- someone else may abuse them and there will be no one to protect them again. The emergence of psychological symptoms and disorders result from the impact of the abuse on the child.

SHASHANNA'S STORY

I want to start my story of childhood sexual abuse at the end, in Victory, instead of the beginning, in misery. You see, after all I endured as a child, my Heavenly Father gathered me close to Him, showed me His church, and gave me the family I never had. Through obedience to His commandments and a deep desire for a pure life in Him, I have been healed (yes, miraculously healed) of chronic, painful and

31

dangerous medical and psychological conditions. I wake up without the physical and emotional pain I had suffered every day. It sometimes is still so surprising to me to feel so good for the first time in my life.

Ok, let's go back to the ugly beginning. I was born into a confused and violent household which, according to my mother, had one child too many. She made sure that every day I knew that I was the one too many. You see, in my mother's mind it was MY fault that she couldn't have a bigger house, or go back to school, or most importantly, escape her miserable life that included me. I know from my earliest memory that my mother hated me, and I created in my own mind the reasons why. I was "worthless, a terrible mistake, the ultimate waste of space". Even as a tiny child I could never look in mirrors because I was disgusted by what I saw and I "knew" my mother was right to hate me so much. As one might have guessed, I was on my own very early in life. My older siblings had learned that they could copy my mother's treatment of me because children act according to what they see. I don't blame all of their cruelty on them. They were children of violence and abuse too.

I remember the day I decided I could not trust anyone. It was a turning point for me because I doomed myself to a life of isolation and fear. I thought I needed to control every minute of everything in my life so I could feel safe, but I lived this way for decades and I never felt safe. I just spent all my time missing out on life as an adventure and on what the Power of God can do. The Power and Love that would truly make me happy. I'll get back to that later.

I have my first clear memory of my father raping me when I was about 4 years old. My mother took my siblings with her on an errand, leaving with a strange look of ominous delight in leaving me alone with my father. They hadn't been gone five minutes when I heard my father's footsteps approaching my room. Now you must understand that my father was a violent man, unpredictable and cruel. It always seemed he needed control of all those around him and he got it by intimidation and physical violence. We all lived in fear of setting him off, so the tension was palpable every waking minute. To a degree he got what he wanted, but his life was just as miserable as the rest of us.

I go back to that terrible memory. He came in my room and took something from me that should have been valued and protected. He used his tiny daughter to live out his sick fantasies and nearly destroyed her in the process. I remember the pain I felt on so many levels and the only thing he said to me was on the way out of my door. He kind of growled, "Don't tell your mother", and closed the door behind him. I heard his footsteps fading away. I remember feeling so shell shocked and the pain of the physical violation only made me realize that my mother already knew.

As I grew up, this scene and others like it were repeated often. All these horrible "secrets" kept me from reaching out to anyone, but I never felt anyone would care anyway. I went to school with black eyes, bruises, and hunks of hair ripped out, and no one seemed to notice or care. I now realize that some people may have actually cared, but just didn't know how to help me. I was also what I would now call –"odd", which repels people. I can't hate anyone for their lack of action to help me.

I was so alone for so much of my life. My father worked outside the home and made good money for that time. But he squandered and mismanaged money so we never had enough. My mother worked inside the home for most of her marriage, and what tiny bit of money was eked out to her, she mismanaged. The children were the ones to suffer. At times we had to go days without any food, and we went without coats in cold weather. Our clothes were always second hand, the wrong size, and poorly made. Now the fact that we had something should be appreciated, but I already was "the girl" who couldn't relate to anyone, had no friends, and was overweight. To factor ugly, ill-fitting clothes into the mix made my life outside the house almost as miserable as inside the house. The stress and pain of my existence along with the self-loathing I had developed, caused me to develop Bipolar Disorder. This condition, which is often activated by extensive and prolonged stress, was undiagnosed and untreated for decades. I just did not understand why I was so deeply sad at times. And other times I didn't feel the need to sleep much, and felt smarter and faster than usual. I again dealt with this alone. Then I started having small seizures. I didn't have anyone to trust so I just dealt with everything alone.

When I was a teenager my parents finally divorced. It was so wonderful that my father, and the men he brought home with him at times who also sexually abused me, were not going to be there to hurt me any more. Though unfortunately, I was still going to be living with my mother and siblings who tortured me both literally and figuratively. I suffered with medical conditions I did not understand. Every day I woke up in despair, and the loneliness was only exceeded by the confusion. I often thought of suicide, but "knew" I couldn't do it right, so I feared the consequences.

As soon as I finished high school, I married a wonderful boy I had been dating. I wanted out of the "family home" so badly. I didn't get help for what had been my secrets for so long, because I just didn't think I could. I assumed I was defective and had to accept what all my family said was true. Unfortunately the nice boy I married had some of his own issues and we were completely unprepared to make a life together. At that time I was unable to have any healthy relationships—especially one as intense as marriage. So we divorced about one and a half years later. This marriage was also on rocky ground because we did not honor God's commandments before we were married. We did not invite God the Father, Jesus the Son, and the Holy Ghost into our individual lives, or into the marital relationship. And we did not rely on the strength of the Godhead as we tried to minister to each other in our wounded states. I don't blame anyone, but I do wonder what might have been—if I had had parents who loved me and led me in a Christian life.

As I continued through my life, the deficits I felt from my childhood became my banner. I honestly didn't know things could be better for me, and that with God's Truth and help, I could make good things happen. Instead I continued hating myself and everything about me. I would actually cover the mirrors wherever I lived so I wouldn't have to see disgusting me. I struggled with food issues all my life and remained "fat enough" to keep people at a distance. I moved from one bad relationship to another without stopping to figure out what I could do to change the outcome.

I was so damaged and felt so hopeless. As a young adult I tried twice to commit suicide. The first was a clumsy attempt that got me a stay in the psychiatric ward of a hospital. From that I gained the knowledge I "needed to do it right the next time". The second attempt was well planned. I had a new bottle of 90 pills of medicine to treat my anxiety disorder by lowering my blood pressure. I wasn't scheduled to see anyone for days. I took the whole bottle of medicine and went to bed...... So why am I here? Because God loves me and wants me on this earth. There is no other explanation. That's when I started believing in miracles. This was another turning point in my life.

Sometime later I entered counseling and began to see how many beautiful things were in the world. I met some great new people, but still struggled so with my own feelings of worthlessness and self-hatred. During that time I suffered a minor stroke. I was very blessed--- because only my abilities to read and write were taken from me. Later, I was given lots of ways to get around that.

I also started searching for the Truth with all my mind and heart. I explored different religions and spiritual beliefs. This was the time I was so very blessed with a new counselor. She was a Christian and very spiritual person who embraced the latest therapy techniques for helping people heal. When I first met her I was reserved and fearful. I couldn't find one good thing to say about myself or my abilities. I was still broken, but I found hope.

We worked together in therapy for several years. With her knowledge and kindness, I began to heal and find my real self. I even found the strength and tenacity to banish the abusers from my life. I've kept them away and will continue to do so as long as it is what's best for me. Because of the new therapy techniques my counselor taught me, it's as if I carry a therapist with me and can continue the healing whenever there is a need.

Once I reached a place of growth that I had never experienced before, another great miracle happened and my whole life converted to great joy. My conversion story begins when my car broke down in the middle of a small town in Alabama on a freezing January day. While I stood looking under the hood of the car, I heard a deep voice behind me ask "Need some help?" Not sure what to expect, I turned around and saw two young men in short sleeves with ties on and name tags.

They talked to me with such kindness and then took a look at the car. One of the men with a bit of experience with cars gave me several suggestions that would solve some problems. They then offered to fill a container with water for me at a nearby business where they were doing some service work. I asked them, "Aren't you freezing?" and they said, "Nah, we're from Utah." Well it took three trips back and forth before my car had enough water, but these young men never seemed impatient or annoyed. They asked me if I would give them my phone number so they could check later to see that I got home safely. They had introduced themselves as missionaries, and after seeing them in action, I felt safe in giving them my number. They did call later to check if I was safely home.

A few days later the missionaries called again to see how I was and to ask if they might come visit with me. I already had some trust in them, so I agreed to the visit. When they came to my home, they explained they couldn't come inside, but we could visit on my front stoop. Though it was January, and I wasn't from Utah, I wanted to talk with these amazing people. This began four and a half months of visits on my front stoop.

The missionaries let me ask a million questions without ever losing patience. I told them from the beginning that I already believed in God, and would never join their church, but they said that was fine and kept coming over. Whenever they would visit, I would feel a peace and happiness that would last for hours after they left. I so looked forward to their visits, the discussions, and the answers to every one of my questions. They gave me a Bible and other spiritual books to read, but since I had lost the ability to read after my stroke several years earlier, they got me CD's to listen to. After studying these books they asked me if I accepted Christ as my Savior and Lord, and I did. Then they asked if I wanted to be baptized. I agreed and they were very excited. They made arrangements for my baptism, which was on April 27, 2009. I truly believe that on that day I was changed down to my very molecules. Everything, literally everything, in my whole life changed: How I saw the world and how I felt about everything. What I wanted in life. What was important now. Never in my life was I truly happy until then, and since then my life has been filled with so much joy. I have been healed through worshipping and obeying Christ. My ability to read and write miraculously returned to me. I have been healed of Diabetes. I have become able to sleep deeply and well, all night through, regularly for the first time in my life. I have new friends and a new family through my church fellowship. I am learning who I really am in Christ's eyes.

The misery with which my life began and continued for so many years, has been changed to a happiness I didn't know was possible. Yes, I was viciously abused my whole childhood, and much of my adulthood. No, my life has not become all it might have been had I been raised in a loving and secure home. My Heavenly Father, however, has made a whole new life for me and it is beautiful. Abuse is a terrible curse and plague in the world today, but the Love and Truth of God breaks this curse, and replaces it with healing and happiness wherever you are and whatever your circumstances.

CHAPTER 4

EMOTIONAL/PSYCHOLOGICAL DISORDERS

WHILE EVERY CHAPTER in this book speaks of the damage caused by child sexual abuse to the child's mind and emotions, this chapter will focus on 5 of the most common psychological illnesses the victims experience: Major Depressive Disorder; Bipolar Disorder; Generalized Anxiety Disorder; Panic Disorder; and Post Traumatic Stress Disorder. Just for clarification, you need to know that ANY human being can develop one or more of these disorders in an adaptive response to significant trauma in their life, as a child or an adult. The National Institute of Mental Health (NIMH) in 2008 estimated that one-half of the USA population will suffer from a type of Depression or Anxiety in their lifetime. Over thirty years ago the estimate was one-tenth of the general population would have an emotional or mental illness. Increased stress in our lives, the mobility and instability of the family unit, more accurate diagnostic tools, and more people seeking professional help have led to the increase in numbers.

<u>Major Depression, also called Clinical Depression</u> is an overwhelming condition that affects the thoughts, emotions, body, and spirit of the

patient. There are degrees of Depression, and if the person does not get professional help, the condition can become worse and last for months or years. The risk of suicide makes Major Depression a health issue that needs treatment to prevent a fatality. We know that even excessive acute stress or severe chronic stress can cause a person's normal brain chemistry to become depleted and malfunction with Depression. A depressed person no longer feels like their normal self. They find it extremely difficult to function in a usual manner partly because of the severe fatigue mentally and physically that they suffer. Having no energy day in and day out is like a car with no gasoline. Thinking slows down, problem solving ability stops, negative and self-defeating thoughts dominate the person, they withdraw socially, and feel hopeless and helpless.

The chemical imbalance of the depressed state can be treated with the correct antidepressant medication that is a good fit for the individual. The goal of the medication is to reduce the depressive symptoms and help the patient get to feeling their "normal best self". Medication that causes the patient to feel doped up, too sleepy, too hyper or agitated, physically ill in some way, or emotionally numbed out—is not the right medication for that individual/is not the right combination of medications/or is not the right dosage for that person. Antidepressant medications are NOT addictive, though to get off of some of them the patient's physician will need to wean the person off to prevent side effects.

Depression needs to be treated not only with medication, but also with psychotherapy. In The Divided Mind, (2006) by Dr. John Sarno, he states "Treating anxiety or depression without in-depth psychotherapy is poor medicine, and may even be dangerous….These affective states are reactions to powerful emotions in the unconscious mind that are threatening to become conscious."

Bipolar Disorder (also called Manic Depression) is described as: The presence of one or more Manic episodes or Hypo-manic episodes along with Depressive episodes. This is a distinct period of abnormally and persistently elevated, expansive, or irritable mood, lasting at least four days in Hypomania to at least one week in Mania, or longer, with 3 or more of the following symptoms: inflated self-esteem or grandiosity; decreased need for sleep (feels rested after 3 hours or less); more talkative than usual or pressure to keep talking; racing thoughts; distractibility; increase in goal directed activity at work, school, or socially; agitation; excessive involvement in pleasurable activities (buying sprees, sexual indiscretions, foolish business decisions).

The Manic or Hypomanic mood alternates with the presence of one or more Major Depressive episodes, as has previously been described above. The "mood swings" of Bipolar Disorder can vary in intensity, duration, frequency, severity and mixture of moods. The mildest form of Bipolar Disorder is Bipolar Type II, with the Hypomanic episodes rather than the more severe Manic episodes, though the Depressive episodes can be just as severe. The more severe Bipolar Type I is readily noticeable by both the patient and their family or physician. Bipolar II is not as observable, and is often misdiagnosed as just Major Depression, Recurrent—and then not treated correctly with medication. About 70% people with Bipolar Disorder tend to have a lot of anxiety. Also, those with Bipolar Disorder tend to have a higher rate of suicide attempts than in these other disorders.

Natalie was so sick and tired of the Depression that left her dragging, barely, through her days. This was countered every few months by racing thoughts, talking rapidly non-stop, sleeping only 2 hours at night, or not at all for several days. During the "fast" phases she would spend all her paycheck on clothes before she realized what she'd done. She'd feel so agitated and enraged at times that she thought she might lose it and hit someone.

She had lost 2 jobs over the past 3 years as her symptoms got worse and more frequent. Thank God a friend had told her of their relative who'd gotten medicine and counseling for the same issues, and was doing so much better. Natalie made herself go see her physician. He diagnosed her with Bipolar Disorder and referred her to an outpatient clinic for counseling.

The therapist worked with Natalie on ways to manage her life more effectively and the importance of staying on medication long term to have a stable life. It came out that Natalie's father probably had Bipolar Disorder as well. He used to have rages when she was a child, beat her mother, and molested Natalie for a year when she was little. With the help of the meds and counseling Natalie was able to be much more "normal", successful at her job and worked at healing from the past abuse.

Anxiety is experienced by everyone in coping with life and in learning new skills while developing adequacy and efficiency. Anxiety is felt on a physical level with increased heart rate and breathing, tightness in the throat or chest, knotting or queasiness in the stomach, and mild shaking or tremors in the hands, knees, or voice. It is also felt on a thinking/emotional level as fear, worry, confusion, uncertainty, apprehension, and terror. We will look at 3 types of Anxiety Disorders commonly found in victims of child sexual abuse: Generalized Anxiety Disorder; Panic Disorder (and Panic with Agoraphobia); and Post Traumatic Stress Disorder (PTSD).

Generalized Anxiety Disorder (GAD) is characterized by chronic anxiety, exaggerated worry and tension, even when there is little or nothing to provoke it. People with this disorder can't seem to shake their concerns. Their worries are accompanied by physical symptoms of fatigue, headaches, muscle tension and aches, difficulty swallowing, trembling, twitching, irritability, sweating, and hot flashes. This can interfere with the person's daily functioning and enjoyment of life. While the person may sometimes have realistic concerns, they fret and worry almost all of the time, finding it difficult to relax. This can affect their sleep, appetite, and social relationships.

Panic Disorder has the essential feature of the presence of "Panic Attacks", also called "Anxiety Attacks". This is described as a period of intense fear in which 4 or more of the following symptoms developed suddenly and reached a peak within 10 minutes: Accelerated heart rate, palpitations, sweating, trembling or shaking, shortness of breath, smothering, choking, chest pain or discomfort, nausea or abdominal distress, dizziness or faintness, chills or hot flashes, feelings of unreality or of being detached from oneself. The first Panic attack so overwhelms and shocks the person that they fear they may be "losing their mind" or "having a heart attack". People frequently go to Emergency Rooms to see if they are having heart problems. Most often they are examined and told their heart is fine, they are just stressed out. Now the person becomes terrified of having a Panic attack in public where others see them or while driving their car.

This chronic fear can develop into an additional Panic Disorder in which the person is diagnosed with "Panic Disorder with Agoraphobia". This is anxiety about being in places or situations from which escape is difficult, embarrassing, or impossible. The person avoids these situations or endures them with great agony. Agoraphobia involves fears of being outside of the home alone, in a crowd, standing in a long line, being in a public place, and traveling in a car, bus, train, or airplane. The person often restricts their travel and social activities severely. Some people rarely are able to leave their home. This prevents them from working outside the home, going to school, going to church, going to a store, and going to a medical facility—except in an emergency. The result is the person becomes crippled by the Panic Disorder with Agoraphobia and limited in the daily function and enjoyment of their life.

Post Traumatic Stress Disorder (PTSD) is an anxiety disorder that can develop after exposure to a terrifying event or ordeal in which grave harm has occurred or was threatened. Nightmares, flashbacks, numbing of emotions, depression, rage and being easily distracted along with persistent frightening thoughts and memories of the trauma occur. The trauma continues to intrude with sight, sound, smell, or body sensation memories in its victims. (Some professionals misdiagnose these phenomena as being the same as visual, auditory, olfactory, or kinesthetic hallucinations, which they are not. The person is not out of touch with reality when these somatic trauma memories occur). Again and again the person relives the life threatening experiences they have suffered, reacting in mind and body as though such events were still occurring, even years after the trauma happened. People with PTSD wonder why they can't just forget or get over or let go of the memories and feelings of the trauma. Friends and relatives say "Why don't you just forget about that? It happened 30 years ago!" ignorant of the facts of how the human brain stores traumatic experiences and freezes them in the mind.

Why does the human brain freeze traumatic memories and physical sensations, repeating them over and over when triggered, re-traumatizing people over and over.....often for a lifetime if they don't get professional help? Extensive research into the biological and psychological functioning of the brain shows that the most primitive and ancient part of our brain, the "Reptilian brain", promotes mankind's survival at all costs. This function served well in millenniums past when a human encountered a life-threatening situation…such as a Saber-tooth tiger, or a cave man enemy in a homicidal rage. Humans did whatever they could to survive using the most basic coping mechanisms of "fight, flight, or freeze". Animal studies show us that animals have these same mechanisms for survival. Yet, they do not usually get PTSD. Their innate instincts quickly diffuse the intense energy that was generated in reaction to the dangerous event. It is thought that humans also used to have this instinct. In modern times, however, most humans have lost touch with those instincts that let them rapidly let go of intense energy emotions. Instead, what happens is that the old brain continues to operate with hyper-vigilant attention to avoid or prepare for similar life threatening events. The results often produce ongoing physical and psychological aftershocks which become maladaptive by staying "stuck" or "frozen" in the memory. Without the interventions of some of our newest, miraculous kinds of therapy, people sometimes carry the feelings of the trauma with them forever.

Not everyone who experiences a traumatic event will develop PTSD. What distinguishes those who do not is still a controversial topic….but there are many clues. Factors that decrease traumatic stress appear to include preparation when possible, successful fight, flight or freeze responses, developmental history, belief systems, prior experiences, internal resources, and social support (family, friends, & community).

Somatic (body) disturbance is the core of PTSD with accelerated heart rate, cold sweating, rapid breathing, heart palpitations, hyper-vigilance constantly, and hyper-startle reaction. When chronic, these somatic symptoms can lead to severe sleep disturbance, appetite disturbance, sexual dysfunction, and difficulty concentrating. These symptoms can be triggered by an internal cue as well as external reminders of the trauma.

In Post Traumatic Stress Disorder it is an individual's subjective interpretation of the event that determines whether it is traumatic to them or not. A traumatic event creates psychological trauma when it overwhelms the person's perceived ability to cope, and leaves the person fearing death, annihilation, mutilation, or psychosis. The individual feels emotionally, mentally, and physically overwhelmed.

The circumstances of the event commonly include abuse of power, betrayal of trust, entrapment, helplessness, pain, confusion, and loss.

The most devastating form of traumatic stress occurs when care giver's become the threat. When the father is also the raging alcoholic abuser; when the mother is also the source of incest or physical abuse, the child feels there is no safe place from the outside world.

Other problems associated with PTSD are:

Self-blame, guilt, and shame—victims blame themselves, believe what their abuser told them about their low-self worth, and feel inadequate when they are not able to function normally and fulfill current responsibilities.

Aggressive behavior toward oneself or others—feelings of rage at not having any control during the trauma and not being able to control the PTSD symptoms causes some victims to lash out at others. This can cause job problems, marital and relationship problems, and loss of friendships. Or, the victim may be self-destructive and have behaviors that repeatedly sabotage himself.

<u>Problems in relationships with people</u>—people who have been through traumas often have a hard time feeling close to others or trusting people. They may feel detached and find it difficult to feel or to express positive feelings. They may isolate themselves socially which tends to make their problems worse. Adults who were abused as children often have huge problems with emotional intimacy and healthy sexuality, in that their first experiences with closeness and/or sex were emotionally painful and distorted.

<u>Problems with identity</u>—different types of traumas may change the person's world, such as loss of someone significant, or loss of a career, and the PTSD symptoms cause them to not be able to function in ways they normally did at home, work, and with others. They feel they are like a different person then they were before the trauma happened.

<u>Problems with self-esteem</u>—the symptoms of PTSD and shame about the trauma, worse if they were abused by a caregiver, can cause a person to feel worthless, bad, stupid, ugly, incompetent, not good enough. They may feel they are "damaged goods" and that they are permanently damaged.

It began happening in her classes in high school right after she watched that news story about the girl being kidnapped and sexually abused. Tracie felt a little dizzy and weird, then she saw images of people dressed strangely around a big campfire--- on the walls in her class, like watching a movie. She felt absolutely terrified! "Am I going crazy?" The weirdest thing was she could actually smell the fire right then.

Tracie didn't tell anyone. She just kept these haunting incidents to herself, worrying about her sanity and what the "horror movie" meant. Then the night terrors started. Unspeakable images of torture to animals and people at some ritual meetings in the woods. She'd wake up drenched in sweat, heart thudding and hands shaking. "What's happening to me?"

She finally felt getting help was less frightening than things continuing this way. She went to one of the high school counselors she liked so much. Trembling as she tried to express these terrifying events of the past couple of weeks, Tracie finally blurted it out. Ms. Smith hugged and comforted her and scheduled her to see a therapist the next day.

As it turns out, Tracie wasn't crazy. She began to regain memories of being taken for hours at a time by a neighbor to a place where these cruel, inhumane things had happened. Her aunt would be babysitting her and her siblings while her parents worked. The kids would play outside for hours in the neighborhood, making it possible for the neighbor to say she was taking Tracie to the store for a while. The neighbor knew her aunt was lax as long as the kids came home by 5:00 p.m.

The horrible abuses of her childhood were ready to be healed and Tracie had to get professional help to heal. She was so grateful later that the therapist used therapy techniques that made the healing process move quickly and really worked to put the misery behind her, growing stronger and more confident than she'd ever been. Tracie decided to become a therapist herself to help others recover from abuses and traumas.

The most remarkable new psychotherapies are now able to help people with these Anxiety Disorders to reduce or even permanently release these debilitating symptoms in short term treatment. These will be discussed in the last chapter of this book.

We know that the Word of God describes people having these emotional/psychological disorders even in ancient times. We also know that God's Will in His Word is for us to be able to conquer the underlying fears, insecurities, and incorrect thinking that are at the root of these emotional/psychological disorders. And though many of these disorders have biological factors involved, God is able to change us on every level—spiritual, mental, emotional, and physical.

Chapter 12—about healing will show us how to apply God's Word with His promises and miraculous healing power to our lives. And amazingly, the newest sciences—Quantum Physics and the New Biology, explained in that chapter--describe how the miracles God promises to believers CAN and DO happen. So stay tuned in for these incredible Biblical and scientific truths.

SARAH'S STORY

The story of the childhood sexual abuse that I experienced contributed to me having staggering feelings of inferiority, immense insecurity, difficulty trusting others, and distrust of my own perceptions. The perpetrator of my abuse was an adult male that my family knew. As far as I can remember, the overt physical part of the molesting began when I was 9 years old. That went on for at least a year. After that, the covert part of the abuse continued for many years, with the perpetrator looking at me with lust and making inappropriate, humiliating and threatening remarks. I never told anyone about the abuse as a child because I was absolutely terrified.

A primary impact from the child abuse in my life was a stronghold of Depression that began to affect me in childhood and grew significantly when I was a young teenager. Depressive thoughts such as "I'm worthless, I feel inadequate, I'm powerless, I feel hopeless" robbed me of energy and peace. The recurring episodes of deep Depression caused me to have chronic fatigue which is so debilitating mentally and physically. When you don't have enough energy to think well, to be alert and present in your environment, and you feel like you don't have enough energy to even take a shower to get ready for school or work....you are crippled in your daily functioning.

Social withdrawal is another symptom of Depression that often affected me. Because you are so tired 24/7, can't think correctly due to your brain processing slowing down, and you have multiple negative thoughts that make your life look dismal, you just don't feel like being around other people. This can keep you from going to church, going to sports events or other social activities, and even make you unable to go to work or school. Even in your own home you may withdraw by staying in bed all day, or by not talking to family members.

When I was 16 I had moved to a new city and new high school. My family was undergoing many severe stressors at that time and I sank into the deepest Depression I had ever experienced. Because my parents were dealing with so many problems and were weary from their own struggles, and because I didn't know what was wrong with me-- I just coped by sleeping more when I could, and by resorting to compulsive overeating to escape my misery.

I began to feel emotionally numb much of the time, and to wish I were dead. I don't remember planning suicide, but one Saturday morning when I was 17, I felt such despair that I went to the bathroom, locked the door, and took a razor out of the cabinet. I looked at my wrist and thought weakly, "That's going to hurt", and then I looked into the mirror over the sink. For a minute I seemed to step outside of my body and look at the severely depressed girl in the mirror, who looked so terribly sad. I felt a flood of compassion and caring for that teenage girl in her suffering…. And I put the razor back and never came close to attempting suicide again. I know that Christ was with me in that room that day, and He is the one who showed me His love, compassion, and caring.

I am thankful that I have been willing to seek professional counseling many times in my life to find ways to decrease depression and anxiety, and increase my self- esteem. Antidepressants have also been a huge blessing to me. They helped me feel more "normal", like myself again, and to have the energy to live. Without therapy with caring, competent professionals helping me, I would have suffered much more and taken longer to heal from the effects of the childhood abuse. I know the Lord has led me in all steps of my healing and I am so grateful.

It wasn't until I was 27 that I gave my life to Christ, though I had believed in God and prayed for many years. I began going to a Bible study group with a friend where I started reading the Bible and discovering the truth about life in His Word. The truth that Christ loves me unconditionally and will never leave me. I continued to learn and grow in my wisdom about His grace and how He can and will provide for all my needs. I just need to ask, believe, and receive. And thankfully the Lord guides me in becoming more the person He created me to be, and showing me how to make my life fuller and happier along the way.

CHAPTER 5

SLEEP DISORDERS

D EAR READER—PLEASE DON'T dismiss this chapter as unimportant just because it is short!! Everyone I've ever met who was sexually abused as a child has had a Sleep Disorder of some kind. Getting regular solid healthy sleep is a serious requirement for physical health and mental/emotional health. Many people go to their medical doctor with sleep deficiency as one of their complaints. While they may be prescribed a "sleeping pill" medication, the sleep disorder is often not fully corrected and they continue to suffer with inadequate sleep for years, or become hooked on addictive sleep meds. And the cause of the sleep disorder from Post Traumatic Stress is not treated or healed from only a pill.

Chronic poor sleep can cause or worsen Depression, Anxiety, and multiple physical health conditions. Severe lack of sleep can actually cause a person, anyone, to have a psychosis—being out of touch psychologically with reality. So getting a good 6—8 hours of sleep each night is of high importance.

The child or adult victim of childhood sexual abuse commonly has difficulty going to sleep or staying asleep. Due to the hyper-vigilance from PTSD, the child consciously and subconsciously tries to stay on guard, alert, on edge in an effort to protect themselves from further abuse. They also have a startle reaction in which any loud noise or sudden movement can cause them to bolt awake. They may resist going to sleep to try to "keep safe".

Frequent terrifying nightmares from the PTSD cause the person to wake up nightly, or erratically. Poor sleep only increases their anxiety and fears. Many victims sleep only a couple of hours nightly, never being fully rested, for years.

Some people with Depression sleep too much as a way to escape from their despair and painful circumstances. Yet no matter how much they sleep, they still do not feel rested. The severe chronic fatigue continues. At least this person receives some sense of escape—even peace—when asleep and not dwelling on their misery.

One of the first things I focus on with patients who are sleeping poorly is to work with them and their physician to get them sleeping well soon. This is best accomplished without addictive medications if possible. There are several good sleep aids that are not addictive and help people sleep well even with chronic physical pain.

There are a variety of types of therapy techniques that can help patients to heal emotional causes of the sleep problems and be able to regain the ability to relax and sleep well regularly. Some of these will be discussed in the last chapter on the New Therapies at the end of this book.

Though Charmaine was on several medications—an antidepressant, a mood stabilizer, a beta blocker to decrease her anxiety, and a strong sleep aid, she rarely slept more than 2 hours at night. It was the massive anxiety she suffered with as a result of the torment of the crazy, abusive family she grew up in. It was a miracle that she had even lived to 18 years old, not just because of what she endured at home, but because of her desire to die but not completing any suicide attempts.

For years after she left home, she continued to sleep poorly. Even now with these medications and the remarkable results she was having from counseling, she couldn't relax and feel safe enough in her own little home to sleep. Then her counselor taught her how to calm herself and decrease her anxiety with a self-help tool. She used the Emotional Freedom Techniques daily, several times a day to relax herself. Miraculously, when she got her mind and emotions to relax, her body's chronic pain decreased too. Then she taught herself how to do simple, basic meditation. This also helped her relax her mind and body. After a while, she found herself sleeping 5 hours a night, 7 hours a night, and feeling safe in her house and in many social situations for the first time in her entire life. These changes in Charmaine's health and mental health gave her the motivation and courage to find a church to seek God more and perhaps make a friend. And that's exactly what she did.

CHAPTER 6

EATING DISORDERS

T HE CREATOR OF the Universe made our bodies to live on a variety of food and liquids for nourishment and pleasure. Our bodies were designed to intuitively know when we need fuel, what kind of fuel would be best at that time, and how much to eat without overeating. Just as continuing to pour fuel into your car tank when it is already full causes waste, so does feeding our body too much fuel repeatedly cause waste in the form of fat and extra size to appear on our body. Then we are at risk of developing physical health problems and emotional distress of self-consciousness and low self-esteem. While it is said that 65% of adults in the USA are currently overweight, when our self image and the words we say are "I am fat and feel ugly" we are vulnerable to one of the biggest prejudices and forms of rejection known to humankind, and to feeling Inferiority and Insecurity about our body. So, of course, common sense would guide us to eat reasonably and exercise adequately to maintain our ideal weight, size, shape, and health. BUT....Oops!! The underlying negative emotions in our Subconscious Mind dictate our true beliefs and steer our actual behaviors. That is why most diets even coupled with exercise will fail to produce a lasting change in our behavior and bodies. We must get help to actually re-write the computer program in our brain which has convinced our subconscious mind that we can survive best by overeating and staying overweight.

Compulsive Overeating in children and adults who were sexually abused children is a major type of unhealthy coping skill. A sister disorder, Bulimia, claims 70% of those diagnosed as having been victims of sexual abuse. The severe anxiety that feels life threatening which accompanies the trauma of sexual abuse and the PTSD that follows it, feels unbearable to the victim. Then the brain/body figures out that overeating, binging, and compulsive overeating cause chemical and behavioral changes that temporarily reduce stress and increase calmness.

A recent edition of The Curves Magazine, (winter 2011) states " 'Researchers are looking at even deeper causes of emotional eating with the use of sophisticated brain scans and studies on how stress hormones affect mood and cravings. For example, stress releases glucocorticoids, hormones that turn up the volume on your emotions and cause many people to eat more. Glucocorticoids also cause a rise in insulin, which can signal your body to take in more sugar…. This increases your craving for sweets and fats rather than healthier choices', says Mary Dallman, PhD, a professor emeritus of physiology and psychiatry at the University of California, San Francisco. Then to seal the deal, sweets cause a rise in Dopamine and Serotonin, neurotransmitter chemicals in the brain that create a sense of calm. But Dopamine is also associated with addiction, and though its release may be subtle after you eat a sweet, it's enough to tap into your reward and pleasure system."

The overeating often takes place in a rapid fashion…where even the intense chewing is a part of decreasing the anxiety. Once the person is in the habit of overeating large amounts of food, especially junk food, they tend to do it "in secret". The feelings of having to hide the habit of getting their "fix" adds to the already huge shame the victim of sexual abuse feels.

<u>Bulimia</u> is described as: Recurrent episodes
Recurrent episodes of binge eating characterized by both of the following:

1. Eating in a specific period of time (within any 2 hour period) an amount of food that is definitely larger than most people would eat during a similar period of time and under similar circumstances.

2. A sense of lack of control over eating during the episode; inappropriate behavior in order to prevent weight gain, such as self-induced vomiting; misuse of laxatives, diuretics, enemas, or other medications; excessive fasting; or excessive exercise; self-evaluation (self-esteem) is unduly influenced by body shape and weight.

Candy hated herself for the gross habit of vomiting up everything she ate. But, it was the only way she found to keep her weight close to normal. Those stupid nerves of hers—causing her to crave sweets and binge on horrible amounts of junk food several days each week. She'd gained 20 pounds in 3 months until she figured out about making herself vomit. She hated her body when she felt fat.

She didn't realize the compulsive eating and vomiting were related to her most shameful secret…more shameful than the binging and purging. That when she was 12 she was molested by a life guard at the community pool near the locker rooms. She was so embarrassed, humiliated, and mortified that she never told anyone.

Then when she got into high school she saw the life guard, who was a senior there. He leered at her and smiled in a creepy way, so she always tried to avoid him. Later she found herself being nervous a lot and sometimes crying at home. The overeating began later….and was a core focus of her life now. She felt if she could be slim and pretty enough, her peers would like her and she'd be happy finally.

The person with <u>Compulsive Overeating</u> or "<u>Binge Eating</u>" has behavior similar to the description of above, except they do not purge or compensate excessively in other behaviors. They may try many diets and try exercise off and on in attempts to control their eating and to lose excess weight, but they do not go to the extreme elimination behaviors of the Bulimic.

Nevertheless, the adult/child sexual abuse victims who are either the Compulsive Overeater or the Bulimic, have patterns of obsessing about what they are going to eat and when they will be able to eat in the "feeding frenzy" to accomplish the relief they seek. Then the Bulimic tries to eliminate the food or effects of the food in some way, while the Compulsive obsesses about the next diet and weight loss program. Much of the addictive behavior of these Eating Disorders takes place in the thinking and planning, all of which distract from anxiety and stir up substitute anxiety.

Mandi had tried countless times to lost the extra 30 pounds and stay at her best weight and size. But it had been many years since high school and she still hadn't conquered her problem. It was so frustrating to keep hoping, trying a new diet, forcing herself to exercise several times a week, losing some weight, then gaining it all back. She knew she used food like a drug—to soothe her unhappy emotions and get her through too much stress. Unfortunately, it seemed much of her life was stressful. Well, at least she had quit smoking a long time ago. Surely she could somehow overcome this problem too. She was so sick of obsessing about either what food she wanted to eat or how soon she could lose a lot of weight and feel more confident. If only she could get motivated enough to discipline herself to get the detested weight off and keep it off. Her counselor, who had helped her so much decrease depression, feelings of shame, and low self-esteem related to the sexual abuse she experienced at age 7, referred Mandi to a therapist who used a technique called Psych-K.

In Mandi's first session she worked on changing her subconscious mind to feel safe about being her ideal weight and size; to believe that changing her lifestyle to one of fitness was achievable without struggle; and that at her ideal weight she is strong and capable of relating to a healthy, stable, loving man. She was fascinated by the Psych-K Therapy. A month later she was amazed that she was eating a healthy 1200 calories a day, working out 5 days a week regularly, and it was EASY. She didn't use food the way she had for so many years—to self-medicate bad feelings. WOW! She was so happy with her motivation, determination, and changing body.

Another eating disorder which is not as common in victims of childhood sexual abuse as Bulimia and Compulsive Overeating, is Anorexia.

<u>Anorexia is described as:</u>

Refusal to maintain body weight at or above a minimally normal weight for age and height; intense fear of gaining weight or becoming fat, even though underweight; disturbance in the way in which one's body weight or shape is experienced (such as seeing oneself as fat when in fact one is emaciated), or denial of seriousness of the current low body weight; absence of at least 3 menstrual cycles due to lack of healthy body weight.

In her newest book, "<u>Women, Food, and God</u>", 2010, Geneen Roth notes that out of all the addictive behaviors a person can have, the food addict is the most difficult to solve because we truly cannot be abstinent from food and liquids forever—as we can learn to be from alcohol and drugs. She goes on to wisely proclaim that "Spiritual hunger can never be solved on the physical level"…And it is Spiritual hunger that is behind our Eating Disorders no matter what the other causes/emotional wounds are.

Self-hatred becomes a trap for the child abuse victim with an Eating Disorder because underneath the low self-esteem and shame of the eating and weight issues, is the shame of feeling "dirty, bad, and betrayed" that goes with being a child victim. While the person's Conscious Mind is trying to deal with the eating/ weight problems, their Subconscious Mind is working to keep them feeling Safe…in which case the Eating habits briefly decrease anxiety and the extra weight feels like a Safety net, keeping possible perpetrators at arm's length.

In "<u>The Course on Weight Loss</u>", 2010, by Marianne Williamson, her brand new book on the spiritual/emotional healing of compulsive overeating and overweight, she says:

"Spirit alone has the power to positively and permanently reprogram both your conscious and subconscious mind. ….This course is not about food but about spirituality—the quest for a power that is greater than your own…"

"The overeater has a delusional relationship with food, imbuing it with power it doesn't actually possess. Perhaps you've subscribed to the magical belief that eating affords you comfort and strength, even when you are eating food (or an amount of food) that can only hurt you. The overeater forms an idolatrous relationship with food in which powers that belong only to God have been ascribed to something else."

The two books mentioned here are fabulous for helping victims of sexual abuse who have eating/weight issues to understand themselves better, and to learn new visions and methods for healing those disorders… through faith, and receiving the LOVE of God.

CHAPTER 7

ADDICTIVE DISORDERS

S TUDIES OF WOMEN with substance abuse problems reveal that about 90% of women who have addictions to alcohol and/ or drugs were sexually abused as children. Studies indicate that 2/3 of all patients in drug/alcohol treatment report they were sexually abused as children. Obviously, people use mind altering substances to try to block Post Traumatic Stress symptoms from the child abuse, as well as symptoms of other types of Anxiety and Depression, and feelings of Inferiority and Insecurity. Unfortunately, these attempts at "self-medication", to relieve their suffering, works temporarily at best, and plunges the victim/survivors into the new kinds of Hell of chemical addictions. An addiction to anything unhealthy promises Heaven but delivers Hell.

The sexual abuse child victim suffers alone, unable to share their painful feelings with anyone. Addictions are about avoiding and covering up overwhelmingly painful emotions, and attempting to change to have "good feelings" for a while. The temporary relaxation, decreasing of anxiety and depression, and escaping into a "high" that provides quick relief becomes psychologically addictive as well as chemically addictive. Of course when the high wears off, the abuse victim feels worse and soon seeks to gain the desired high again. It appears that the acquiring and using of substances to get high is the aim of the alcoholic or addict…but what they are actually wanting is to escape their chronic pain… and to try to reach a higher level of consciousness…happiness, joy, peace, feeling loved… in a quick fix.

As we'll see in chapter 9 on "Intimacy and Sexual Issues" many people who were sexually abused as children and teens, have tremendous anxiety about not only overt sexual behavior such as foreplay and intercourse, but also about the whole process of interacting with someone that is a potential romantic interest, thus leading many adult victims to use alcohol or drugs to decrease that anxiety. Otherwise, they feel they would not be emotionally or socially able to withstand the inherent "tension" of flirting, seduction, and sexual behavior. That dynamic tension, rather than being a powerfully pleasant experience, is unnervingly painful to the victim of childhood sexual abuse.

Amy discovered the benefits of alcohol at age 16. Under its influence she became outgoing instead of depressed and quiet, funny instead of serious or boring, and confident instead of self-critical. She liked herself better and it seemed other kids liked her better too after she'd had a couple of drinks. In the beginning, she was able to flirt and make-out with boys without much hassle.

Now, at age 25, Amy couldn't drink without getting drunk. And once she'd had a sexual relationship with one of her boyfriends at age 18, she'd become likely to go to bed with a guy whenever she was drunk, even a "one night stand'. Her drinking was no longer cool. She often felt out of control. And she knew some of her friends from college considered her to be too wild and promiscuous. This wasn't how she wanted her life to be. She'd thought that when she got out of college and on her own that she would be so much happier. But the depression, shame and confusion from the effects of her grandfather sexually abusing her as a little girl, had followed her. Now she also carried shame for being a drunk and never having a relationship with a man who truly cared.

The intrinsic low self-esteem and sense of shame, feeling like "damaged goods" as a person, also contributes to the victim relying on a substance outside of themselves to give them courage and false self-esteem in social situations. John Bradshaw, in his landmark book "The Family" states that "Incest is usually more shaming than any other form of abuse…and dramatizes in the most powerful way the tragedy of the abandoned child." Feeling inadequate, "less than" others, and often lacking in appropriate role modeling of healthy social relationships, the victim wants social interaction but feels they need the "lubricant" of the relaxing or energizing effects of their substance of choice.

Denial is one of the primary symptoms of addiction and the alcoholic/ addict lies to themselves in the face of massive evidence that their addiction is creating huge problems in their life…and in the lives of those close to them. Efforts by others to try to control the alcoholic's/ addict's use of substances is futile, as progressively the addiction becomes the most important focus in their daily lives. The alcoholic/addict believes they cannot live without the substance and the desired high it brings. Often in order to get someone to seek treatment and begin the recovery healing process, an intervention by several people closest to the addict must be organized and conducted to shock the addict with confrontation of facts from all facets of his life.

Few humans can maintain sobriety for long periods of time in isolation from others in recovery. The "will" or willpower of the addict has been defunct for quite some time and trying to stop and stay clean with no help or support results in "white knuckling" efforts. Of the very few humans who do manage to stay sober from substances on their own, most usually do not deal with the underlying psychological facets of the addictive disorder, resulting in the person being a "dry drunk". Unresolved emotional issues such as resentment at others, anger issues, low self-esteem and the flip side—arrogance, rigid thinking, negativity, and codependency issues of being domineering or passive cause ongoing relationship problems.

Rarely do victims of sexual abuse decide to face and deal with their abuse issues and work on healing the trauma of the abuse while they are actively abusing alcohol or drugs. It is only in the light of staying in a recovery program such as Alcoholics Anonymous (AA) or another spiritual program with fellowship and guidance, that the victim seeks to heal the root causes of their addictions. The 12 step programs of

AA, Narcotics Anonymous (NA), Cocaine Anonymous (CA) etc. have had the most significant success since 1935 of treating and helping millions of people get and stay clean and sober. While these programs do not promote a specific spiritual view, they do focus on the inability of the addict to heal themselves, the need for a "Higher Power", and the fellowship of others in recovery to provide an anonymous stable environment for safety, hope, and progress. Many recovering alcoholics and addicts who were atheists or agnostics, do come to the revelation of the truth of God and of Jesus Christ through healing in the 12 step programs.

Dr. David Hawkins, internationally esteemed psychiatrist, in his book "Power vs. Force", 1995, says Alcoholics Anonymous and the other 12 step self-help programs that are offshoots of AA, provide tremendous spiritual power and influence, helping millions of people heal and lead healthy, productive lives..." which hitherto nothing on Earth including medicine, psychiatry, or any branch of modern science had been able to do." Only rarely reported individual spiritual experiences prior to the advent of AA had been able to free one from an addiction.

Sammy was a party guy—always drinking the most, always had pot, sometimes had cocaine. He liked being considered wild, crazy, and tough. He welcomed fights, with his quick temper and effects of the alcohol loosening his judgment. He won the fights because it gave him a place to unleash his pent up anger on others. And he was vicious.

Underneath his macho, carefree, careless exterior no one would guess he hid the secret of his father beating him and raping him from ages 8 - 12. By 12 years old Sammy- was large enough and enraged enough to hold a baseball bat in his hands and fiercely threaten his father when he came into his bedroom—for the last time. "If you ever touch me again, I swear I'll kill you". The look in Sammy's eyes and clenched teeth when he spoke convinced his father he meant it. ....
That night Sammy swore to himself, no one would ever hurt him or betray him again.

For those involved with victims of sexual abuse who suffer from a chemical addiction, participating in the 12 step program, Alanon, is extremely helpful to learn effective ways of coping with the addict's behavior and to receive the support and fellowship of others connected to alcoholics/addicts. While a family member or friend of the addict cannot change the addict's behavior, she can learn in Alanon how to live in more healthy ways.

Often people with addictions, and those closest to them, feel hopeless about the addict ever maintaining sobriety and living a good life. While many who seek rehab treatment do relapse over and over, the ability to stay clean and sober exists through the healing of God, and through the support and guidance of such spiritual and practical 12 step programs.

CHAPTER 8

RELATIONSHIP ISSUES

OUR RELATIONSHIPS IN life are the most important criteria that determine our level of happiness. Studies show that the people who are the most happy have fulfilling and meaningful relationships with significant others in their life.

The adult who was sexually abused as a child, and who has not obtained treatment or healing, tends to have immense difficulty trusting anyone. When the abuse was a form of incest, the trust is shattered even more. The child abused by a family member is thrown into the realm of not trusting those in the family to protect him, or be honest with her. If you can't trust your family, your home isn't safe, and your foundation is shaken. The ones who are to teach the child how to view herself and the world are untrustworthy, so the child tries to decipher alone how to proceed to survive in this seemingly hostile world. But, no one has taught the child how to value and trust her own perceptions and feelings. Since incest is not discussed openly, due to its severe taboo in all cultures on the planet, the child victim is not allowed to have her truth recognized, seen, or voiced. Nor does she receive any emotional support to deal with the pain of the incest. So the child begins to feel that her own perceptions are "crazy" and to doubt her memories when they arise to the surface of consciousness. The survivor tries not to think about the past abuse, and denies that it even happened. Plus the child's own subconscious mind tries to repress the horrid memories to help her survive.

This background forms a shaky foundation for relationships on a casual level and on a deep level. The child/adult victim isolates emotionally and develops Codependency patterns in relating to others. John Bradshaw in his book, "The Family", (1988, 1996) defines codependency as "a dis-ease of the developing self causing various degrees of de-selfment....It is a loss of ease with oneself, a feeling of inner emptiness, a state of not being at home with oneself."

Codependency can be understood as a characteristic of an adult who is contaminated by childish dependency needs—great insecurities. Dr. Bradshaw goes on to say that "Codependence is the core of addictiveness. It is a dis-eased form of life. Once someone believes that his identity lies outside of self, in a substance, activity, or another person, the victim has found a new god, sold his soul, and become a slave... Codependency is at bottom a spiritual problem. It is spiritual bankruptcy."

In codependent relationships the victim of childhood sexual abuse either tries to dominate and control others; or is passive and non-assertive through fear and insecurity, allowing others to control him. A relationship of equal respect and open communication is impossible in a codependent relationship. Manipulation through degrees of dishonesty rules the relationship. It takes courage, integrity, and maturity to be honest and straightforward—without feeling too vulnerable or attacking, judging, and trying to control the other person.

Tanya depended on Frank, her husband, for income, doing the most strenuous chores at home, and helping with the kids. Yet she nagged him most of the time for just about everything. They argued, yelled, and fought often. When they drank it got worse.

Frank tried to argue and fight less, and get closer to Tanya. She rarely let him. If he was compromising, she would totally run over him......
He knew she'd been abused as a child—physically and sexually. He guessed that her desperate need to be in control and to push him away stemmed from that. He tried to get her to go to counseling with

him—or alone—, but Tanya said "I don't want to talk to anyone about my past." ....Frank eventually had to leave or completely lose his identity and his sanity.

Beth Moore writes about the Stronghold of Insecurity in her book "So Long Insecurity", 2010, "The insecure person also harbors unrealistic expectations about love and relationships. These expectations, for themselves and for others, are often unconscious. The insecure person creates a situation in which being disappointed and hurt in relationships is almost inevitable. Ironically, although insecure people are easily and frequently hurt, they are usually unaware of how they are unwitting accomplices in creating their own misery."

In order to have the ability to know what kind of person they are attracted to physically as well as emotionally, mentally, and spiritually, and to choose a healthy mate, a person needs a foundation of a strong sense of their own identity. They also need to have at least reasonably good self-esteem. Quantum Physics shows us there is a Law in the Universe called "The Law of Attraction". This law is the way like (similar) energy patterns—attract like energy. Positive energy patterns of thoughts, beliefs, emotions and actions attract like positive energy. Negative energy patterns of thoughts, beliefs, emotions and actions attract like negative energy. A survivor usually has low self-esteem in many areas of their life. Thus, on an unconscious level of energy they will attract people who also have low self-esteem. One person may exhibit theirs as passiveness, while another person may exhibit theirs as being controlling. The passive one is often a "people pleaser", doing too much giving to the partner, allowing others to take advantage of her or even abuse her. The dominant partner exhibits their insecurity by trying to exert control through orders, criticism, demands, possessiveness, and withholding of attention, money, affection, and being abusive.

Bobbie Jean couldn't understand why she always ended up with the same kind of man—someone abusive. Her first husband had turned out to be so violent that he threatened to not just beat her but kill her. Thank God she finally took her friend's advice and went to a shelter to get away from him.

Her second husband mostly emotionally abused her, though he pushed her occasionally when enraged. He always criticized her, told her she was fat and stupid and no other man would ever want her. She believed him and that kept her from thinking she could leave and have a better life. But when she went to counseling secretly, she began to learn she was a worthwhile person just because she was a child of God. She started to like herself, and to feel smarter and more attractive.

She came to realize the childhood sexual and verbal abuse she endured had caused her to see herself as worthless and unlovable, which caused her to attract abusive men because that was what she was familiar with. When she understood that husband # 2 would never change, she divorced him as well.

Now Bobbie Jean was staying away from men for a while. She was working at a job she really liked and her self-esteem was growing. She found a church she loved that taught such positive truths from the Bible, about God's love, forgiveness, and empowerment through her redemption in Christ. She had faith in God to transform her into a woman who could someday have a healthy loving relationship with a Godly man.

Codependency results from dysfunctional relationships and results in dysfunctional relationships. Seeking outside guidance through counseling and/or 12 step programs (many of which are offered in churches and have a specifically Christian thrust) will assist individuals and couples in healing. This is less difficult when they seek professional counseling through their pastor or Christian therapist, who can see both sides of the issues, as well as clarify God's Word for the couple. Praying together out loud can also make a huge difference in the couple seeking God's will, understanding each other, and compromising for the benefit of both. They can become capable of emotional intimacy which requires mutual respect, including self-respect and the ability to self-soothe.

Starting with our relationship with our Creator—the love, trust, honor, praise, worship, and intimate communication with Him—form the basis for all other relationships, including the one with our Self. When we are connected to the Lord we learn from His Word how He sees us, who we are as His child, how He created us to live abundantly, and how he designed us to relate to other people. His Word describes how to relate to others in ways that bless Him, them, and us. Jesus summarizes the 10 commandments into 1 new commandment in John 13:34 "Thou shalt love the Lord your God with all thy heart, with all thy soul, and with all they mind; and love thy neighbor as I have loved you." This means all of the earlier 10 commandments are upheld in this 1 new commandment of Love. A person who realizes how awesomely and unconditionally God loves us, who truly loves God and is obedient to His commandments….does not commit adultery, steal, lie, etc., though they may at times have temptation. When we are disobedient and get out of God's will, which is revealed in His Word, we have "missed it" or sinned. We need to admit it and confess it to God. Then we choose to repent (change, turn around) from the error of our hearts, words, and actions. God promises to forgive us and teaches us how to forgive others. We gain freedom and open our life for more blessings and miracles to flow to us from God.

MARK'S STORY

I was 9 years old. He was my Sunday school teacher and lived in my family's neighborhood. So when he asked me and my parents if I could come to his house on a Saturday to work on a project for the class, we all agreed. Little did I know—it would be the beginning of living in Hell for me.

When my mother dropped me off at his house, his wife and kids were there. He and I went into his garage where he had a wood working shop area. Soon his wife and kids left to go on some errands. He asked me if I wanted a coke and of course I said yes. So we went into the kitchen. He got out 2 cokes and said "Let's watch the ball game for a few minutes while we drink our cokes." After we sat on the couch a few minutes, he moved closer to me and put his arm around me. I felt a little uneasy—but, hey, he was my Sunday school teacher that my family and I'd known for over a year.

Suddenly he started touching me in my private parts. I was shocked, terrified, and didn't know what to do. I tried to push his hands away and cried "Stop it," but within a few minutes or less, he was raping me.

I was in pain and felt so ashamed, powerless, and scared. He told me if I told anyone he would kill my dog, Toby, who I was always talking about. When my Mom came to get me that day, I didn't say anything. I was so relieved to see her and to get to my house. ... I tried to forget all about it.

I wish I could say that it never happened again. But he was still my Sunday school teacher, so I saw him every week. I hated to be around him and my stomach always felt queasy. The second time it happened, he had asked my parents if I could stay after church with a few other kids and help clean up after a Fall Harvest Festival at our church. I was too scared to say no with him right there in front of my parents and me.

No other kids stayed to clean up. He attacked me and raped me again at the church. Then he showed me some photos he had taken of me and Toby playing out in my yard. And he showed me some photos of some dead dogs. I got the message..... He raped me several more times that year.

I felt like a zombie—trying to live my regular life--- go to school, make good grades, play with my friends, and be with my family. But, I always had the terror and the humiliation and the worry of what HAD happened, and WHEN would it happen again. I didn't understand how God could let this happen to me. I stopped really believing in God— until my Dad's job transferred him and we moved to another state. The abuse ended. I absolutely did thank God for that.

I tried to just forget about it, put it behind me. For a few years it seemed like it had been a distant nightmare. Then, as a young teenager, I began to have fears that because a man had forced me to have sex, that meant I was now gay. I was so confused. I began withdrawing from people, especially other teens. I felt if they knew the truth about me, they wouldn't want to hang out with me. Other than going to school (which became a struggle for me because I had a deep depression) and having to go to church with my family (which I was totally confused and angry about), I mostly stayed home and listened to music in my room. My parents worried about me, but somehow I kept making good grades, and I never got into trouble anywhere, so they would back off and leave me alone.

I didn't date until I was in my early 20's because I felt ashamed and inadequate around girls. I didn't learn a lot of the regular teenage social skills because I was so isolated for all those years. I noticed I got especially nervous and had panic attacks anytime I went somewhere that mostly men hung out—hardware stores, barbershops, auto repair shops. I couldn't stand being around a lot of men I didn't know when I was by myself.

When I was at college, I went to hear a speaker talk about the effects of sexual abuse on children and how it keeps on hurting them even long after the abuse stops. She also told about medication and new counseling techniques that could help a child abuse survivor get better, and maybe even heal. So, I built up my courage and went to see a counselor.

The therapy definitely helped, along with the medication a Dr. prescribed. My depression decreased, my nightmares of the abuse stopped, and I felt more ok about myself. My counselor recommended that I go to a Celebrate Recovery program at one of the local churches, where they meet weekly and have support and learn about Christ's healing available to believers.….. I had gone to church sporadically since I'd left home after high school. (I hadn't been able to become an atheist due to my early exposure to teachings about God's love and mercy, but I still had a hard time trusting God and trusting a church.) I prayed about it, and decided to try it.

I found out there was a church that had not only Celebrate Recovery for people with alcohol and drug problems, but also for people who had been physically and sexually abused as kids. I was so nervous the first night I went. I kept wanting to back out. But—the small group of people helped me feel comfortable—even "normal", in spite of all I'd been through. And they had their own stories to tell.

Over time I made huge progress in getting over the past abuse and learning how to be more happy and healthy in the present. I know now that God didn't abandon me during that horrible abuse. He was with me helping me survive the whole time. Satan tempted my former Sunday school teacher who committed the evil, and Satan used my wounds to keep me trapped in misery, negative beliefs, lack of faith in God, and shame about myself for years. But, I know God led me to hear the speaker and to show me that Christ wants to heal me and can heal me.

I can't believe how good my life is now. I have several close friends, a good job, a great church, and no depression. I'm even in college, thanks to the counselor and medication, going to a church with Celebrate Recovery and I am engaged to a wonderful young Godly woman who loves me and knows all about me. I can only thank the Lord for all this --my Savior, Redeemer, Healer, and Provider. Thank you, Jesus.

CHAPTER 9

INTIMACY AND SEXUAL ISSUES

OUR SEXUALITY IS something sacred that God created. He intended for sex to be a beautiful way to create a new life, continue our species, and to bring a couple together in a loving, intimate, wholesome relationship. Child sexual abuse is an Evil---that grossly distorts the child's perceptions of emotional intimacy, identity, and sexuality. Abuse twists God's intention of healthy loving sexuality into something the victim believes is terrifying, fearful, ugly, dirty, confusing, shameful, and painful. Without healing from the abuse, victims universally have problems in experiencing normal healthy sexuality.

Some victims have the added confusion that their body responded sexually to some of the sexual acts by offenders. A 'trauma bond' occurs where body pleasure and abuse are paired in the victim's mind. This causes the survivor to unconsciously be attracted to people who will abuse them. This survivor is often especially self-critical because their body did respond to touch.

Some people avoid romantic relationships and sex altogether, feeling that any sexual feelings are bad. "Sexual Anorexia" is the lack of sexual appetite or denial of normal sexual drive. Some victims become compulsive in their sexual thoughts and behaviors, developing excessive appetites. This can turn into "<u>Sexual Addiction</u>" in which the abuse victim obsesses about sex and engages in risky sexual behavior (affairs, promiscuity, and/or deviant sexual actions).

Patrick Carnes writes in his book, "<u>Sexual Anorexia</u>", (1997) "Our sexual behavior is a core expression of who we are…We do not change fundamental personality traits or beliefs when we become sexual. Issues that we have in general, we will also have sexually." Many abuse survivors believe that they are physically unattractive and undesirable. This, along with other aspects of low self-esteem, shame, and feeling inadequate can keep them from even trying to have romantic relationships. Others may date and marry, but have overwhelming anxiety about any sexual interaction. Some women survivors love their husbands but fear and hate sex. They may avoid affection and flirting as well--- to avoid any sexual encounter. Or they may "do their duty" having sex with their spouse but not enjoying it. This of course presents problems with emotional, physical, and spiritual intimacy in the marriage. Some women survivors of childhood sexual abuse do get to where they can relax more and enjoy closeness with their husband. Even then, flashbacks of the abuse may occur, rendering the wife now unable to be in the present moment and enjoy sex with her husband. Some women can enjoy some aspects of sex with their mate, but are unable to relax enough to reach orgasm, which causes stress for the couple and feelings of inadequacy on both the male and female's part.

Some survivors have been able to have sexual relations before marriage with some physical and emotional success. However, once they get married they perceive that now they are not free to be sexual—but have a "duty" to be sexual with their spouse-- and they suddenly feel trapped. This can cause triggering of flashbacks of having been forced to have sex and being trapped as a child victim.

Sally loved Joe and looked forward to their wedding. They had enjoyed a good sexual relationship before marriage, but she was glad he was the only one she'd slept with. He was a great guy who really loved her and she knew she was so lucky to be with him.

On the day of the wedding Sally's father—whom she couldn't stand and feared—told her "Now you have to do your duty as a wife and have sex with your husband." Sally didn't understand why those words caused her torment and revulsion. But after their honeymoon was over, when she and Joe settled into their own apartment and got into the daily routine of work and married life, Sally began to not want sex with Joe. She felt immense anxiety now even thinking about having sex, and felt she had no choice, because she was a wife. Joe wasn't angry, just confused and worried. He felt the emotional and the physical intimacy fading.

Because they loved each other so much and knew they'd had a good sexual relationship before, they both agreed to go for marital counseling after the first year of their marriage. There the memories of being abused sexually by her father when she was 8—10, flooded back. Now it made sense why Sally disdained and avoided her father always, and why his sneering words on her wedding day had her feeling forced to have sex, rather than having freedom of choice, as she felt she did before the marriage. She had been forced to have sex with her father as a child. Those smoldering old feelings affected everything about her sexuality in her new marriage. With some EMDR Therapy, Sally was able to heal from the abuse and learn to feel comfortable with her husband sexually.

Some adult victims can behave sexually and enjoy sex, but not in an emotionally intimate relationship. They feel free to be sexual only in casual relationships. The world has told us for many decades now that it is fine to have casual sexual relationships since we have good birth control and "sexual liberation". When we acknowledge that sex is still a life or death matter -- it creates life, and some sexually transmitted diseases bring death and destruction—and recognize the heart breaking pain that adultery and promiscuity bring to couples and individuals, we can see why God wants parameters around our sexual behavior.

Marianne Williamson says in "A Course in Weight Loss", 2010:

"Casual sex is not wrong just for some moralistic reason; it's wrong because it violates something profound and extraordinary by cheapening its value…We have been left exposed over the last few decades by a hell-posing-as-heaven of sexual license, leaving us feeling not so much liberated as unprotected."… Earlier she states: "Modesty is not just some old fashioned we-don't-need-this-anymore value; it is a <u>spiritual energy</u> that dignifies and protects female sexuality from both abuse by men and misuse by women."

It is a common unhealthy coping skill of survivors to use alcohol or drugs excessively to decrease their anxiety in anticipating and participating in sexual activity. Before they can relax at all they must numb their trauma emotions. Male victims of child sexual abuse may also suffer performance anxiety resulting in pre-mature ejaculation or difficulty in reaching a climax. Couples in which one of the pair is a survivor of abuse may experience great difficulty developing a healthy sexual relationship in which both people want sex and emotional intimacy, and are able to be mutually satisfied. Communicating about how the history of abuse affects the victim now can begin to help the couple understand each other's perceptions and enlighten the non-victim partner. However, often the victim dreads telling the partner about their past abuse and some have never told their spouse even after years of marriage. Being able to talk about the abuse in a non-judgmental, compassionate way can open a door to help healing occur. Individual therapy for each of them and marital/sexual therapy can also help. An excellent book to read about helping couples heal marital sexual relationships is by Dr. David Schnarch called "<u>Passionate Marriage</u>", (1997). He was the first marital therapist to combine sex therapy and marital therapy together, in his unique system called the "Sexual Crucible". He has had amazing results working with couples in monogamous committed relationships. He helps them to heal the emotional and sexual problems in the relationship, and to create the most enjoyable sexual intimacy ever. Dr. Schnarch believes we each have the capacity to experience great spiritual moments in a committed healthy sexual relationship.

Thirty year old Paul loved his wife, Tammy. At least he thought he did. It's just that sex in their marriage was feeling like a chore and obligation to him rather than a fun escape. The frequent cheating he did, secretly (often just a few rendezvous with a new woman--- nothing serious), were his way of letting off steam from life stressors. He tended to go for older women and felt powerful in being able to seduce them and mesmerize them with his sexual prowess.

Paul didn't like to think this pattern was related to his mother's "use" of him sexually as a boy. That secret he kept hidden under a lid, where it simmered, waiting for the day the lid would blow. And blow it did—when Paul came home one night to find Tammy, all her clothes, and their dog gone, with divorce papers sitting on the kitchen table.

God created us as sexual, sensual creatures to enjoy affection, touch, and intimacy as well as to ensure procreation. It is interesting that the world usually thinks of sex as something "dirty". The Truth is that sex is an exquisite gift God gives us to share and enjoy with someone we love in a trustworthy, covenant relationship. Because healthy sexuality is created by God and intended to bless us, we can know that He is fully able to heal us from the harm imposed by childhood sexual abuse. He is able to restore us to healthy sexual thinking, feelings, and functioning. As with any healing process, some healing may occur quickly, and other healing may occur in progressive steps.

CHAPTER 10

FINANCIAL ISSUES

ONE OF THE signs of being under the effects of a CURSE is chronic financial insufficiency and/or poverty. Our Father God promises His children that He will provide a "full supply" which means "more than enough money and provision to meet all their needs and to give into His Kingdom here on earth". The Word of God says in Philippians 4:19 "My God shall supply all your need according to His riches in glory by Christ Jesus." He knows we have need of food, clothing, shelter, transportation, medicine, education, and other material supplies. Since He promises to supply our needs according to "His riches in glory by Christ Jesus", that means He has unlimited resources from which to supply our needs. God is not affected by the local or world economy (things in the "natural world"). He is the Creator of the entire Universe and He is Supernatural power.

How does being a victim of childhood sexual abuse affect the survivor's life in financial matters? The curse of false negative beliefs about WHO they are—ashamed, rejected, betrayed, damaged, unworthy, unloveable, inadequate—twist the victim's self-image. Those negative beliefs are the opposite of what God tells us about who He sees us to be as His children.

The erroneous beliefs shape the victim's sense of identity and cause them to create turmoil and chaos in their life repeatedly. Quantum Physics shows that our thoughts, beliefs, feelings and actions attract energy that is similar/alike to the energy we give out. Chronic low self-image and feelings of failure are oppressive and cause Strongholds of negative behavior patterns. With the symptoms of Major Depression, Bipolar Disorder, Post Traumatic Stress Disorder, Panic Attacks, etc. common to survivors of child abuse—accomplishing life's normal tasks of getting an education, obtaining and maintaining a good job/career, having a stable loving marriage, and being on top of managing finances—all become huge hurdles to achieve and maintain.

Tim was so frustrated and angry about his inability to build and maintain financial stability and security. For years he had earned a good salary, but they lived paycheck to paycheck. He tried to save money—then the car would break down or one of the kids needed dental work, and there went the beginning of his savings. He felt guilty for not providing more security for his family. Oh, they had a nice home, good cars, decent furniture and clothes. So all looked good on the surface. But he and Kim had almost no retirement invested yet. Every time he had changed jobs and they'd moved to another state, they had cashed in their retirement money to move and get a new house. They also didn't have money saved for the kids' college years...and time was flying by.

Tim felt inadequate and like a financial failure. "I guess I should have listened to my old man's financial advice when I got out of college", but at that time Tim still hated and disrespected his father for sexually abusing him when he was just a little guy, helpless and terrified. "How could I take advice from that imposter—that Monster—even though he was financially successful?" Tim was so ashamed of being abused as a little boy, and now he was ashamed of his chronic financial mistakes. But he would pull himself back up from the despair and search again, try again, and pray for help to change.

Some survivors are so chronically, severely crippled by their emotional and physical symptoms that they become unable to continue to work full time. They may qualify for Social Security Disability (SSD) based on their many medical and psychological conditions. But that is a long road to climb and the SSD income is rarely adequate for a comfortable living. Other survivors may keep working but miss much work due to their emotional and physical symptoms, thus affecting their success. Difficult work situations may cause so much stress that the survivor feels they cannot handle the stress, feeling "trapped" in a miserable work environment....again triggering PTSD feelings of being "trapped" as a child victim.

With their difficulties in choosing an emotionally healthy spouse and in developing and maintaining a good marriage, the survivor may end up divorced once or many times. Statistics show that divorce frequently causes lower income and loss of financial security and stability. Single parents raising children perhaps without child support or without adequate financial help, struggle to make ends meet.

Survivors who became alcoholics and/or drug addicts usually create unstable finances and chronic debt. Even those who are in Recovery successfully may take years of re-building their lives financially. Spending addiction and chronic debting are behaviors that some survivors use to try to change their mood from depression or anxiety to temporary happiness and excitement. As with other "quick fixes" these measures seem to promise a solution but deliver the survivor into a worse nightmare.

The process of learning from God's Word how to be a good steward, to follow His wisdom in attracting and creating abundant prosperity, and managing finances His way, is a lesson many survivors never learned in their family of origin. If the survivor was taught these things in their family or church—but was also abused by someone there—they will often reject even valid teachings which came from the perpetrator.

The oppression of feeling low self-worth and patterns of repeated financial stress and mismanagement are curses Satan uses to keep the survivor's life always insecure and fearful. The belief in the perpetual lack of resources, of "not enough" takes its wear and tear.

Thank God His Word teaches us something very different than those messages, and very different from what the world teaches about money and wealth. The Word says "He is your constant Source of stability." Isaiah 33:6. In 2 Corinthians 9:8 the Bible tells us "God is able to make all grace abound to you, so that in all things at all times, having all that you need, you will abound in every good work."

God tells us we need to honor Him by giving a tithe, one tenth of our all our income. This is not because God needs our money. He has all the money in the universe and created every good thing in existence. He commands this because it is the way we "put our money where our mouth is" by believing and claiming He is our Source and showing we have no other gods before Him. When we honor and obey Him with our top 10% as soon as money comes in to us (the "first fruits"), he expands the other 90% of our income and it goes further. When we don't obey Him in this, it causes us to trust ourselves to provide for ourselves and manage our money more than we trust God. Also people often don't tithe because of fear that they won't have enough money left to pay all their bills. So they are placing their faith in Fear rather than in God and His Word.

In Malachi 3:10—11 the Bible says "Bring ye all the tithes into the storehouse, that there may be meat in mine house, and prove me now herewith saith the Lord of hosts, if I will not open you the windows of Heaven, and pour you out a blessing, that there shall not be room enough to receive it. And I will rebuke the devourer for your sakes and he shall not destroy the fruits of your ground, neither shall your vine cast her fruit before the time in the field, saith the Lord." So God challenges us with saying we can test Him to see if He in fact blesses us.

In Malachi 3:8—9 the Bible says "Will a man rob God? Yet you have robbed me. But you say 'Wherein have we robbed thee?' In tithes and offerings. Ye are cursed with a curse; for ye have robbed me, even this whole nation." So we see that God wants to bless us financially and protect us from Satan and financial harm, but in order to do so it is required that we GIVE to God to honor Him and show that we realize and believe He is our Source of everything good, including all our money, property, and blessings. When we don't tithe…whether out of fear that we won't have enough, or whether out of lack of knowledge, or rebelliousness, or lack of caring and worshipping Him, He cannot bless us as much. This is one of the first and most important steps in building financial security, prosperity, and peace.

Linda was a 55 year old with a professional degree and career, divorced two times, having thankfully reared her 2 kids—almost by herself—except for her mother's help and support in emergencies. She was very intelligent. She knew that. Yet she persistently repeated financial errors over the years. Borrowing money to survive became the habit. Consequently she had little to show for her years of successful work, other than a good house—with a mortgage, and a good car— with a car note.

She blamed herself for her lack of knowledge and discipline in saving and investing. Working, raising kids, keeping up the house, and surviving all those years, had taken its toll. She just hadn't spent the time learning how to manage her money well. She also had a chronic fear of there not being enough money. (This worry never helped bring in more money. If anything it kept her self-defeating pattern going). She was sad that she never had experienced a happy marriage. With her background of being physically and sexually abused as a child, growing up in a home with rampant alcoholism and domestic violence, what could she expect? Not exactly training grounds for knowing how to pick a good husband or be a good wife. And she had never divorced well financially.

Thankfully Linda had found a church where she was learning about God's promises to His children of provision and prosperity. She had never been taught before the ways God shows us how to manifest His promises. Now her life was transforming with her commitment to honor God in tithing, a growing savings account, her car being paid off, and with extra income she was earning with her hobby of selling used cookbooks on Ebay. She had a new habit of speaking out loud several times a day Scriptures of God's promises of abundance, security, and wealth. She constantly thanked God for everything. She praised Him for all good things happening and when something bad happened, she claimed victory over that with her faith in the Lord. The power of her faith in The Word and speaking these Truths out loud both encouraged her and produced changes in her life. Amazing Grace! Linda was doing better financially now than she ever had and she was looking forward to a bright future.

So how do we actually acquire the abundant life God promises us in His Word? We begin by seeking salvation in Christ. Then we trust the Lord and tithe every time we receive money. This is planting seed that God then brings to harvest. We meditate on God's Word, pray (communicating from our hearts to Him) and speak His Word in our minds and out loud. The mechanics of activating our Faith in Him is in 2 Corinthians 4:13 "We have the same spirit of Faith according to what is written "I believed and therefore I spoke". This fits perfectly with Quantum Physics and the Law of Attraction which says that in order to manifest things in our life, we have to imagine what we desire, speak it out loud with strong emotion, and take action that promotes it happening....until it appears. This process is "planting seeds of the Word of God" and we will receive a harvest if we do not give up.

The survivor of child abuse struggles with having a belief that they are unworthy of abundance...that God would actually give it to them. Changing this belief on a subconscious level is imperative. God wants us to have more than enough abundance to meet all our needs and to give into His Kingdom on Earth. And the better stewards we are, the more we can help other people in God's will financially as well as spiritually.

A wonderful book to read or course to take to help get out of debt and build good financial habits and stewardship in practical ways is "Total Money Makeover" (2003, 2007), by Dave Ramsey. Dave tells how he went through great financial times in his 20's, then lost it all through managing his money incorrectly (the way the world says to do). He then rebuilt his finances and life according to God's Word, Will and principles, and became highly successful with stability and security. He teaches people "how to live like no one else, so you can later live like no one else". He has helped millions of people become good stewards and debt free in relatively short periods of time (the average family takes 18—20 months under his guidance). Once people are debt free and have a significant emergency savings fund, Dave Ramsey teaches them how to build wealth with balanced, wise financial methods over time. Besides, his book is fun because of his witty remarks in humorous confrontation, honesty, and mentorship.

CHAPTER 11

LIVING IN A FALLEN WORLD

W E OBVIOUSLY DO not live in a perfect world or child abuse and other horrors would not occur. In order to get to the perfect world—Heaven—we are given the choice by God to choose life or death here on Earth. Deuteronomy 30:15 "See, I have set before you today life and good, death and evil." We have choices because God gives us free will.

We need to face the facts—that in 75% of cases of child sexual abuse, the perpetrator/child molester is someone the victim knows, and is often a member of their own family. We know that some of the people who molest children were sexually abused themselves as a child or teenager. Statistics indicate that only about 1/3 of children, or less, who are molested—become adults who molest other children. Thank God.

Some people who molest one child may never molest another. However, since we don't know who will molest more children and who won't, this is another major reason to confront the abuse as soon as you discover it. If a father sexually abuses his daughters and/or sons, and the abuse is covered up and denied, that father could go on to sexually abuse his grandchildren, nieces or nephews, or neighborhood children. Estimates are that the perpetrator who is an actual Pedophile (not all offenders are) will likely molest as many as 80—100 children or teenagers in their lifetime.

In order to stop the offenders who are committing the abuse and protect the victims, we must use courage and Godly strength to confront the child sexual abuse. We must have the abusers face consequences and have rehabilitative therapy to help them repent and change their hearts and behavior. This will require not only social and legal leverage, but the redemption of Christ for the offender. Because there is so much shame and covering up of child sexual abuse, we have allowed abusers to continue in their behavior and to not have to face the truth of their actions. While this may seem the easier way for them and for their families, it is in fact harmful to them, their families, the child abuse victims, and society at large.

In the Bible the Apostle Paul writes "If anyone is caught in any trespass, you who are spiritual, restore such a one in a Spirit of gentleness. " In James 5:30 we read "Whoever turns a sinner from the error of his way will save him from death."

So it is vitally important that those of us who follow Christ lead others in confronting the abuser in the way God guides us. We must help the abuser acknowledge the truth and accept responsibility for his/her sins. Hopefully, the abuser will experience deep remorse for hurting the victim and hurting other people so much. Then he/she will genuinely repent –- turn around their heart and behavior in a new direction in God's will. With the intensely negative social and legal repercussions to child sexual abuse, the abuser will have to deal with these issues, even if he/she does repent. However, we serve a Holy God with Supernatural wisdom and power, and if the offender has truly repented and committed his/her life to Christ and purity, Christ can do miracles of healing in the offender's life as well.

We must help the victims by being aware, noticing, listening, taking action to protect them, and getting them professional and spiritual help. And we must bring the perpetrators to the Light and Love of Christ. Christ is able to forgive the abuser who truly repents of his/her dark behavior. Then Christ is able to change their hearts and help them LIVE in the Light of God's Will. Just as Christ helps alcoholics and drug addicts to be abstinent and in recovery from their addictions, so He is able to help the abusers to be in recovery. Just as Christ forgives prisoners, redeems those who sincerely turn to Him, and helps them turn their lives around, so can He do the same for repenting offenders.

And ultimately, as Christians, we must forgive the abuser. Forgiveness is the requirement of our Lord who died for each of us and forgives us of our own sins. "For all have sinned and fall short of the Glory of God". Romans 3:23. In Matthew 6: 14-15 Jesus says "For if you forgive men their trespasses, your heavenly Father will also forgive you. But if you do not forgive men their trespasses, neither will your Father forgive your trespasses." Forgiveness does NOT mean ignoring the abuse, pretending it didn't happen, not protecting the victim, or sweeping the crime under the rug. Forgiveness means bringing the darkness of the abuse into the Light. It means having the victim receive spiritual/psychological help, and the abuser receive consequences, rehabilitative help, and spiritual/psychological help.

An article in Oprah Magazine, the May 2011 issue, is on forgiveness and titled "Letting Go." Harriet Brown, the author, quotes Robert Enright, Ph.D. professor of educational psychology at the University of Wisconsin-Madison. He states "The decision to forgive touches you to your very core, to who you are as a human being….It involves your sense of self-esteem, your personal worth, the worth of the person who's hurt you, and your relationship with that person and the larger world." The article discusses studies which indicate that forgiveness lowers blood pressure, improves sleep, decreases depression and anxiety, and increases hope and self-esteem. Actually, forgiveness seems to do more for the forgiver than for the person they are forgiving.

Forgiveness is part of the healing of the victim, and the family of the victim. It is also part of the healing of the abuser, and the family of the abuser. It is not something we can do in our own human weakness. It is Christ living in us and the Holy Spirit working in us that helps us make the decision to forgive. Forgiveness is the most loving and healthy response of our hearts, once we have done the very difficult work of dealing with the wounds from the child abuse. As one of my therapist friends said "There is no such thing as cheap forgiveness."

A final comment I want to make here is about the worldly media push over the past 50 years to make "sex" seem like the most important thing in people's lives, perhaps right after "money". With the majority of TV shows, movies, and magazines promoting loose sexual values, casual relationships, and vulgar language ---a very unhealthy culture exists. Pornography tries to come into our homes via the Internet, our ears are bombarded with rampant cursing in movies and on TV, and we see the promotions of shallow values all around us. Our children, teens, and young adults are frequently brainwashed to think those values and cheap excitement are what makes the world go round. Too many children and teenagers are encouraged or allowed to dress provocatively, wear make up too young, shave their legs too young, date too young, and grow up too fast. They lose the innocence of their childhood formative years.

As followers of Christ we can take a stand against these false values by refusing to watch those TV shows and movies, not buying those magazines, having protective software on our computers, and setting guidelines for dress and behavior with our children. I close with the simple Model Prayer that Jesus taught us to pray in Matthew 6: 9-13 about seeking the Lord's will and forgiveness:

The Lord's Prayer

Our Father in heaven,
Hallowed be Your Name,
Your kingdom come,
Your will be done
On earth as it is in Heaven.
Give us this day our daily bread.
And forgive us our debts, as we forgive our debtors.
And do not lead us into temptation,
But deliver us from the evil one,
For Yours is the Kingdom and the Power
and the Glory forever. Amen.

CHAPTER 12

AMAZING NEW THERAPIES

THERE ARE MANY "New Therapies" that give therapists and patients creative tools for psychological healing that we have never had before. Most of these New Therapies are less than 20—30 years old, yet are still considered cutting edge and are not mainstream. Some of them have had significant clinical research conducted over the years that give scientific evidence of their effectiveness and efficiency. However, because they are not "traditional" therapies, they are not in wide-spread-use yet. Other new therapies are in the early stages of clinical research, yet there are numerous testimonials by patients and therapists as to their ability to help facilitate healing.

Quantum Physics provides knowledge and understanding of how some of these therapies work on the body/brain's energy pathways, to access Subconscious thoughts, feelings, and beliefs and bring them to Conscious awareness. Then often quickly and gently, yet profoundly, the patient is able to "let go" of traumatic memories and body sensations of past traumas. Old negative thoughts, emotions, and beliefs are changed by the patient, on the Conscious and Subconscious levels of the mind, releasing new energy in the present, with healthy new behaviors.

As a therapist I have been trained in three of the newest therapies and use them as a Christian counselor to help patients heal much more quickly than was possible in the past. Amazingly, at times it only takes from one session to twelve sessions to enable the patient to have incredible healing of past traumas. Each of the three New Therapies that I like can be used separately for specific reasons, or can be combined with one or two of the other methods as is indicated for the best precise healing of the individual patient. Each of these therapies helps the patient do much of the healing inside their mind, without having to discuss in great detail the traumas. Of course, some patients want to tell their story because they've never really told it to anyone and they need that catharsis.

All three of the New Therapies I use also stimulate whole brain functioning, based on information from Brain Dominance Theory. Decades of research on "brain dominance" or "split brain research" indicate that each hemisphere (the Left side of the brain and the Right side of the brain) of the cerebral cortex has specialization in different functions. The Left Hemisphere does the following: uses logic/reason; thinks in words; deals in parts; analyzes/breaks apart; thinks in sequences; is ordered/controlled. The Right Hemisphere does these functions: uses emotions/ intuition/creativity; thinks in pictures; deals in wholes/relationships; synthesizes/puts together; thinks simultaneously/holistically; is spontaneous/ free.

While it is natural for us to use both sides of the brain at the same time, sometimes one side of the brain takes dominance over the other, limiting the ability to function as well in the less dominant side. The more emotionally/energetically charged a life experience is, the more likely it will be stored in memory and then we will over-identify with only one hemisphere of the brain when faced with similar experiences in the future. A balanced whole-brain-state is the desired state for changing our old beliefs and behaviors into new more healthy beliefs.

Studies in neuroscience indicate that as much as 95% of our consciousness is actually Subconscious. That is the storehouse for our attitudes, beliefs, and perceptions that we have programmed into our brains since birth. It is from our beliefs that we have perceptions about ourselves and our world. Then we develop actions/behaviors from these beliefs.

There are 3 components of our mind. The first component is the Conscious Mind, the awareness we have on the surface day to day. Our Will in the conscious mind sets goals, judges results, thinks abstractly, and thinks in the past and the future. The brain processing capacity (as a computer) of the <u>Conscious Mind</u> in short term memory is about 20 seconds, of 1-3 events at a time, and it processes information at about 40 bits per second, a few things at a time.

The second component of our mind is the *Subconscious Mind* which we are not aware of much on a daily basis. It operates on autopilot, habitually. It monitors all the operations of our body such as heart rate, digestion, breathing, etc. It thinks only literally, and only in the present time (as if everything that has ever happened or might ever happen, is happening RIGHT NOW). It has our long term memory of past experiences, attitudes and beliefs; can remember thousands of events at once; and processes information at 40 million bits per second. So the Subconscious Mind processes information one million times faster than the Conscious Mind!!

A third component of our mind is called the <u>Superconcsious Mind</u>. This is the highest level of our consciousness. It is also called our Spirit or Divine Intelligence. Scientists call this the "Observer". The Superconscious watches over us like a caring, wise parent. It oversees our growth and development. It uses "intuitive knowing".

The New Therapies allow us to effectively access the Subconscious Mind and the Superconscious Mind while we are awake and alert. With the awareness of the wisdom and oversight of the Superconscious Mind (Spirit within us), the Conscious Mind can re-program, or re-write the self–defeating beliefs that are stored in our Subconscious Mind. This makes changing and healing much quicker and easier than what therapists have been able to do to help patients before now.

The Conscious Mind's God given ability to override the Subconscious Mind's pre-programmed beliefs and behaviors (from childhood experiences) is the foundation of "free will". As a child we download incorrect data and misperceptions which then form incorrect beliefs. The Subconscious is partial to rapidly downloading perceptions in our environment that feel threatening, to protect us. These "traumatic perceptions" can get stuck and replay like a broken record.

There are three types of phenomena that have been studied for many years that support how powerful our thoughts and beliefs are. The Placebo Effect is one type. This is when scientific studies of groups of people who took medications or had surgeries are compared with control groups of people who received a "sugar pill" or "fake surgery". Repeatedly in a variety of these studies, up to 1/3 of the patients who received the fake medicine or surgery improve as much as the people who actually received the real thing. They believed they received the real thing and their body responded to this belief. Vice versa, the Nocebo Effect happens when negative perceptions, beliefs, and chronic negative emotions can have damaging effects on us and our health. Our beliefs act like filters on a camera--changing how we perceive the world around us. Our biology then adapts to our beliefs because our Mind tells our trillions of cells what to do—how to behave. Thus, if a patient is told by their doctor that they have cancer and have only a short time to live, they may take that data in and form a belief that they will die soon, hastening death. Another patient told the same thing, may believe and speak God's Word that she is healed through her redemption in Christ, and become healed.

Another type of phenomena that supports the power of belief is Clinical Hypnosis. A patient who is hypnotized (is in a deeply relaxed state with easy access to the subconscious mind) can stop having the measurable, observable symptoms of a disease when they believe they are disease free. For example, a person who has a rash all over his body, which is itching and unsightly, can have the rash completely disappear--with no more itching, while hypnotized to believe he is rash free.

The third type of phenomena is found in patients who have Dissociative Identity Disorder (formerly called "Multiple Personality Disorder"). There are numerous documented cases of patients who in one personality have medical needs that they don't have in other personalities. For example, in the book and movie "The Three Faces of Eve", a true story of a woman with three separate personalities, Eve needed glasses in one personality and did not in another. A patient may have high blood pressure in one personality, or an allergy, that they do not have in another personality. Mind over matter. Or as Physicist and Author Dr. Amit Goswami states: "It's not mind over matter, it's 'mind = matter'. Not consciousness creates reality, but 'consciousness = reality'."

The three new therapies I have practiced and had great success with are: EMDR (Eye Movement Desensitization Reprocessing) Therapy for the past 15 years; Emotional Freedom Techniques (Accupressure, or tapping on the body energy pathways) for the past 14 years; and PSYCH-K (Psychology-Kinesiology) for the past 9 years. Here I'll give a basic description of these Energy Psychology Therapies and the results that can be achieved with the techniques.

EMDR is a cutting edge therapy developed by Dr. Francine Shapiro, a psychologist, in 1987. She has refined the technology over the years since then. EMDR Therapists are trained by the EMDR Institute Faculty all over the world. Psychology now teaches us that when traumatic events occur, the brain tends to freeze the memories and store the negative highly charged energy. The sensations are locked in the subconscious mind/body and natural healing is blocked. When current events trigger the painful memories of Post-Traumatic Stress, the person is haunted by anxiety, nightmares, panic attacks, depression, rage, and often withdraws from people socially.

Dr. Shapiro observed that when the brain focuses on some type of side-to-side movement (eye movements back and forth, alternating sounds from ear-phones, or alternating touch sensations—such as by hand pulsars), AS the person notices the traumatic memory, the brain unfreezes the trauma and the person can NOW process the data differently. This helps the person quickly, and usually gently, release pent up negative energy of the trauma emotions. The result is the memory is desensitized (does not cause pain any longer) and the brain rarely brings it up because it feels like the traumatic event is truly in the past. Dr. Shapiro and other scientists believe the process is similar to what happens naturally during normal deep sleep called Rapid Eye Movement sleep (REM). This is when we sleep deeply, our eyelids are closed and our eyes move side to side rapidly. During REM sleep we dream, solve problems, deal with stress, and restore balance. Clinical studies of EMDR treatment show that in people who have a single traumatic event (such as a rape, or a bad car accident) it takes only 1-3 sessions to heal. In people who have had multiple traumas (such as chronic child abuse, chronic domestic violence, or war experiences) it may take up to 12 EMDR sessions to heal 77% to 100 % of the traumatic memories and symptoms. This is vastly quicker than the results of traditional types of counseling.

Another important part of EMDR treatment is that the patient does not have to talk about details of the trauma for the therapist and the procedure to help. With a little information, the therapist can guide the patient in healing, much of which happens in their mind. Many people feel that EMDR gives them miraculous results and benefits. The website www.emdr.com gives detailed information about this therapy, clinical studies and results, and the professional training required.

The second Energy Psychology Therapy I've used with very effective benefits is Emotional Freedom Techniques (EFT). I use this technique in therapy sessions and teach patients how to use EFT as a self-help tool. EFT was developed in 1994 by a Stanford educated engineer, Gary Craig, who combined, simplified, and refined several other techniques to work together most effectively. It uses Accupressure, tapping on energy pathways on the body, along with speaking words and expressing emotions in methods that cause rapid changes in emotional states. This is a cousin to Accupuncture, without the use of needles. The tapping creates a subtle healing energy flow that neutralizes negative energy and blocked emotions. This causes energy to become positive and flow smoothly. This results in feeling noticeably more relaxed, positive, and reduces body tension. About 90% of the patients that I teach this tool to have measurable reductions in anxiety, depression, grief, and even physical pain within 5-10 minutes the first time we use EFT.

Earlier contributors to this amazing healing technique were those who discovered and mapped the subtle energy pathways of the body thousands of years ago. The study of Applied Kinesiology by Dr. George Goodheart in the 1950's, Dr. John Diamond, a psychiatrist, in the 1970's, and Dr. Roger Callahan, a psychologist, in the 1980's are all exceptional forerunners to EFT. Gary Craig has donated thousands of hours and millions of dollars to make this technique available freely to people worldwide. The website www.emofree.com has simple instructions for learning and using this technique. There is an abundance of information and articles by health care professionals and lay people about the usefulness of EFT on this website.

The core discovery of EFT is given in the Discovery Statement "The cause of all negative emotions is a disruption in the body's energy system." This cause is a mind-body phenomena which is explained by Quantum Physics—that everything in the universe at a sub-atomic level is made of electro-magnetic energy. When energy in the mind-body is flowing smoothly, we feel good in every way. When energy in the mind-body is blocked, stagnant, or disrupted along the body's energy pathways, negative emotions and physical symptoms occur.

EFT helps a person balance the mind-body energy system while thinking or speaking of the problem causing the negative symptoms. The negative energy is neutralized, causing the person to feel better quickly. The stress level recedes as their adrenaline and cortisol levels drop, and their nervous system is calmer. The new sciences of Epigenetics and Neural Plasticity of the brain explain how EFT can produce these rapid effects. The EFT Manual by Gary Craig, 2010, is a handy small guidebook teaching how EFT works in general, and how to use EFT with specific psychological and physical problems. Dr. Dawson Church, a world renowned psychologist, has written a book, "The Genie in Your Genes" which provides research on the effects of EFT. He also has a website www.eftuniverse.com with much information on using EFT.

Another remarkable Energy Psychology technique I utilize is PSYCH-K (Psychology–Kinesiology). It was originated by Rob Williams, M.A. in 1988. He is author of the book, PSYCH-K… The Missing Peace in Your Life! (2004). He is also the co-host of the DVD "The Biology of Perception…..The Psychology of Change", (2000) with colleague Dr. Bruce Lipton, a world famous cutting edge cell biologist. Rob Williams states, "PSYCH-K is a user-friendly way to rewrite the software of your mind and change the printout of your life! It is a simple and direct way to change self-limiting beliefs at the subconscious level of the mind where nearly all human behavior –- both constructive and destructive—originates."

Rob Williams discusses that "Your reality is created by your 'beliefs'. These beliefs, usually subconscious, are often the result of lifelong 'programming', and represent a powerful influence on human behavior. The subconscious mind is the storehouse for our attitudes, values and beliefs. It is from our beliefs that we form perceptions about the world and ourselves, and from these perceptions we develop behaviors. Often the most effective way to change a behavior is to change the subconscious beliefs that support it. Based on years of split-brain (Right Hemisphere-Left Hemisphere) research, also known as Brain Dominance Theory, PSYCH-K provides a variety of ways to quickly identify and transform beliefs that 'limit' you, into beliefs that 'support' you, in any area of your life. Many people harbor self-limiting subconscious beliefs in the areas of financial prosperity, self-esteem, health and body issues such as weight loss or smoking, as well as relationships and career."

Rob Williams goes on to teach "Your beliefs are the foundation of your personality. They define you as worthy or worthless, powerful or powerless, competent or incompetent, trusting or suspicious, belonging or outcast, self-reliant or dependent, flexible or judgmental, fairly treated or victimized, loved or hated....A great deal of research has been conducted for decades on what has come to be called "brain dominance" theory. The findings of this research indicate each hemisphere of the cerebral cortex tends to specialize in and preside over different functions, process different kinds of information, and deal with different kinds of problems.

The LEFT Hemisphere:
uses logic/reason
thinks in words
deals in parts/specifics
will analyze/break apart
together thinks sequentially
identifies with the individual
is ordered/ controlled

The RIGHT Hemisphere:
uses emotions/intuition/creativity
thinks in pictures/images
deals in wholes/relationship
will synthesize/put
thinks simultaneously/holistically
identifies with the group
is spontaneous/free

"While our birthright is the natural ability to simultaneously utilize both sides of the cerebral cortex, life experiences often trigger a dominance of one side over the other when responding to specific situations. The more emotionally charged the experience (usually traumatic), the more likely it will be stored for future reference, and the more likely we will automatically over-identify with only one hemisphere when faced with similar life experiences in the future."

"Rescripting limiting subconscious beliefs is similar to reprogramming a personal computer. Using PSYCH-K processes, a kind of 'mental keyboard' to your own brain, you can increase 'cross-talk' between the two cortical hemispheres, thereby achieving a more 'whole-brained' state, which is ideal for changing subconscious beliefs. In addition, when right and left hemispheres are in simultaneous communication, the qualities and characteristics of both hemispheres are available to maximize your full response potential. PSYCH-K helps you quickly and easily communicate directly with your subconscious mind, while using methods of whole-brain integration….This changes old self-limiting beliefs into new self-enhancing ones that support you, in just minutes!", Rob Williams shares enthusiastically. The website www.psych-k.com gives more information about this miraculous therapy.

I know that sometimes traditional Christians may have been taught that new psychology techniques are "New Age", ungodly, or even of the occult. Or that since the Bible doesn't talk about EMDR, EFT, or Psych-K, that Christians should not be involved in such things. However, Jesus did not ever fly on an airplane, get lazier eye surgery, or use the Internet on a computer. Yet most Christians do not regard these modern technologies as ungodly or evil. The three Energy Psychology techniques I have discussed are all based in the knowledge of Quantum Physics science, which not only agrees with God's Word but in fact explains many of the reasons why and how supernatural healings and manifestations can happen in the mind-body. The New Biology, discussed in The Biology of Belief (2005) by Dr. Bruce Lipton, is grounded in scientific studies that agree with the newest information in Quantum Physics. Therefore, all of this information is consistent and congruent. It does not contradict the Word of God. In fact, many scientists who were agnostic or even atheist in the past, have been convinced by these sciences that God is awesomely real, powerful, and loving.

One technique the Bible does talk about is Meditation. This has in the past also been considered by some Christians as new age. Meditation has many different forms. Basically it involves the person getting in a quiet place and space, sitting up or lying down, focusing on their breath-breathing in and out slowly and deeply. One of the purposes is to get the mind/thoughts/feelings off of worries and daily tasks, and to relax deeply. Meditation can last from a few minutes to an hour at a time. Studies for many years have shown that Meditation has physical and mental health benefits equal to that of regular exercise, except that this is becoming quiet and inactive at a deep level.

A world famous Chiropractor and Neuroscientist, Dr. Joe Dispenza, travels the world teaching conferences about the magnificent power of our minds and how deep hour long Meditation can be life changing and life healing. In his many books such as "You Are the Placebo: Making Your Mind Matter", (2014) and "Breaking the Habit of Being Yourself", (2012) he teaches and describes how to use Meditation to change your thought patterns and emotional patterns so that you can have physical, emotional, and relationship healing. He and his team have studied and measured brain scans and have numerous testimonials of people experiencing miraculous changes.

My recommendation is that you, the reader of this book, seek a Christian therapist who has expertise in these Energy Psychology methods. Pray, asking the Holy Spirit's wisdom in selecting the right therapist for you. Then get references on this therapist. Next, interview the therapist by phone or in person, to see if you feel comfortable with their character, spirituality, and therapy style. Once you have selected the right therapist, make an appointment as soon as possible. It takes courage and determination to genuinely seek healing, even with these new therapies that are the least invasive emotionally. For those readers who are limited in their ability to pay for therapy, there are places to find therapists who are on a sliding fee scale, or who will see a motivated client for a reduced fee. Also, with these new Energy therapies the number of sessions required for healing is greatly decreased.

God bless you in your healing process, and in His restoring you to the wholeness for which He created you. This glorifies the Father, the Son, and the Holy Spirit and makes you a witness to His love, compassion, forgiveness, and healing power.

CHAPTER 13

HEALING THROUGH CHRIST

"Jesus bore our sins in His own body on the cross, that
we, having died to sins, might live for Righteousness—
by whose stripes you were Healed!" 1 Peter 2:24

HEALING NEEDED BY a survivor of child sexual abuse,
who is a Believer in Christ and the Word of God, is available
to them through their redemption in Christ. There is
tremendous need for spiritual transformation and emotional healing
for survivors. There are at least 40 million adult survivors of child sexual
abuse, in the USA at this time! That is more than ¼ of the entire adult
population of the USA. Of the survivors who are Christians, I would
venture to say that the majority are not knowledgeable about the healing
they can have faith for and claim as children of God. "My people are
destroyed for lack of knowledge". Hosea 4:6. I am amazed that in 33
years of being a Christian and attending several different Protestant
denominational churches over those years, I was not taught—(or else
I did not hear and learn) ALL of the Truth of our right to complete

healing because of Christ's sacrifice for us, and HOW to activate that healing.

Our beliefs, faith, and speaking God's Word of His promises plants the seed for our healing. Claiming Scriptures promising us healing with strong positive emotions activates our healings. "And since we have the same spirit of faith, according to what is written, 'I believed and therefore I spoke' we also believe therefore speak." 2 Corinthians 4:13. We may have an incredible supernatural miracle of healing—such as total immediate healing from cancer, alcoholism, or panic attacks—or we may have a gradual healing, through stages of improving wellness until we are restored to wholeness.

It is interesting that the typical worldly view is that the material, physical substance of things is the most real—that which we can see, hear, touch, smell, taste. What Quantum Physics now proves to us is that at a sub-atomic level of existence everything is made of ENERGY, electro-magnetic energy. Our thoughts, words, feelings, and beliefs are such powerful energy that focused, concentrated attention attracts and creates actual physical matter and circumstances. Thoughts are in fact THINGS!!! We create what is in our material world by first thinking it, visualizing it, intending it, believing it, and speaking it with strong emotion. Therefore, the UNSEEN reality (spirit, mind) precedes the SEEN reality.

The "New Biology" which is based in knowledge we have from Quantum Physics, proves the truth beyond "mind over matter"—that "mind IS matter". In his fabulous book, "The Biology of Belief", (2005) by Dr. Bruce Lipton, he writes of scientific research in biology over the past 30 years, only now being taught to the public. Dr. Lipton states that we now know that our bodies are NOT powerless biochemical machines, and our genes do NOT control our biology. The science of Epigenetics, a new branch of biology, shows that our genes and molecules are controlled by our mind and Spirit, NOT by our DNA as was previously believed. The membrane around each of our 50 + trillion cells in the body is actually the "brain" of the cell, and is a digital computer chip. Our cells are "programmable" just like a computer. The Programmer is our Mind and Spirit!!!

WE are the "drivers" of our own biology! We have the ability to "edit" the data we enter into our "bio-computer cells". Our Mind's energy (thoughts and feelings) directly influence how the physical brain controls the body's physiology. Thought energy tells our 50 + trillion cells membranes (brains) what to do. Positive thoughts (which fuel positive feelings) are Life Supporting. Negative thoughts (which fuel negative feelings) are Life Draining.

Dr. Caroline Leaf is a Christian brain researcher. Since 1981 she has been studying the vast, untapped potential of the human brain. Her book "Who Switched Off My Brain", (2008) teaches how negative thought patterns can be toxic to our body, mind, and spirit...and how to switch our thought patterns to positive, life affirming ones ... "Taking every thought captive to the mind of Christ".

2 Corinthians 10:5. Her research indicates that 87% - 95 % of the illnesses affecting us today are a direct result of our thought life ---due to an epidemic of toxic emotions. She states "The average person has 30,000 thoughts per day. Through an uncontrolled thought life we create the conditions for illness; we make ourselves sick!....Toxic waste generated by toxic thoughts causes diseases…. Change in your thinking is essential to detox the brain."

In "The Spontaneous Healing of Belief" (2008) by Gregg Braden, author and former computer systems designer in aerospace programs, he states "Studies by the Institute of HeartMath have shown that the electrical strength of the heart's signal, measured by the EKG, is up to 60 times as great as the electrical signal of the human brain, measured by the EEG, while the heart's magnetic field is as much as 5000 stronger than that of the brain. What's important here is that either energy field (heart or brain) has the power to change atoms, and we create both in our experience of belief! we may think of the heart as a belief-to-matter-translator...The precise fields of energy that alter our world are created by the mysterious organ that holds our deepest beliefs. Perhaps its no coincidence that the Power to change our bodies and the atoms of matter is focused in the one place that's long been associated with the spiritual qualities that make us who we are: the heart."

The fascinating thing is that all of this AGREES with God's Word. The New Testament of the Bible is over 2000 years old, yet God's wisdom conveys the scientific truths we now find that Quantum Physics proves. The immense power God gives us in our beliefs and words is amazing grace. The Bible says "For we do not look at those things which are (temporary), but at those that are not (eternal)" 2 Corinthians 4:18. So God tells us not to focus all our attention on things as they are in the present, but to focus on things that He promises to us in His Word. That process will help us to materialize positive things and circumstances in our lives. Isn't it awesome that the same TRUTH about God, spirit, the universe, man's thoughts, beliefs, and words... that the Bible has been teaching us for 2000 years is now substantiated by our newest sciences!!

The new physics proves that energy cannot be destroyed—only transformed. God gives us the breath of life at birth, and without our spirit—breath our body is dead. Since Quantum Physics proves that energy cannot be destroyed but transforms into something else, science now proves that there is life after death. God, our Creator and Provider, has the power to create us and give us life in our bodies. Thus it makes sense that He also has the power to heal—restore—renew us in our bodies, minds, and spirits. Our loving Father God raised Jesus's body after He was crucified, buried, and dead for three days. Jesus was and is alive, fully restored, and whole and sits at the right hand of the Father in Heaven. Surely this same Power through the Holy Spirit living in us as born again Christians can heal us on earth now. "By His stripes you WERE healed!" 1 Peter 2:24.

Smith Wigglesworth in his book "Ever Increasing Faith" (1924) states "Our precious Lord Jesus has everything for everybody. Forgiveness of sins, healing of dis-eases, and the fullness of the Spirit all come from one Source—from the Lord Jesus Christ. Hear Him who is the same yesterday, today, and forever as He announces the purpose for which He came: 'The Spirit of the Lord is upon me, because He hath anointed me to preach the gospel to the poor; he hath sent me to heal the broken-hearted, to preach deliverance to the captives, and recovering of sight to the blind, to set at liberty them that are bruised, to preach the acceptable year of the Lord.'"

Dr. Allender in his book, "The Wounded Heart" (1990, 2008) challenges us to seek healing from childhood sexual abuse with his statement "What then is the reason for moving toward the goal of God's embrace? Again, the answer is a hunger for more. God has made us with a natural desire to be as He is: alive, righteous, pure, passionate, loving. To honor what God has called us to be is the reason a man or woman chooses the path of change (healing)."

You may not yet believe in Jesus Christ as your Savior and Lord. Or you may be saved, but have what you feel is weak faith. It is God's desire and power to heal you. Jesus never turned down anyone for healing in the Bible. Know that it is God's Love that brought Jesus to Earth to live as a human, teach and lead us, sacrifice His holy life for forgiveness of our sins, redeeming us--- and this same Love helps you and me to believe. In every weakness God will be our strength. "My grace is sufficient for you, for my strength is made perfect in weakness." How amazing is that?? In Romans 10:10 is the "faith formula", "For with the heart one believes unto righteousness, and with the mouth confession is made unto salvation." 2 Corinthians 12:9. The Bible tells us that "Faith cometh by hearing, and hearing by the Word of God." Romans 10:17. So reading the Bible, listening to teaching and preaching from the Bible, and speaking Scriptures of God's promises to self and others, is what brings faith and increases our faith. The Bible also says in Mark 17:20 "So Jesus said to them 'Because of your unbelief, for assuredly, I say to you, if you have faith as a mustard seed, you will say to this mountain 'Move from here to there,' and it will move and nothing will be impossible to you.' " A mustard seed is very tiny, yet it grows into a very large tree/harvest. It is extremely important to have faith and to develop that faith in God through Bible study, prayer, hearing the Word of God in church, listening to and singing worship music, and being around other believers. "For without faith it is impossible to please God, for he who comes to God must believe that He is, and that He is a rewarder of those who diligently seek Him." Hebrews 11:6.

A wonderful way to increase your faith is to speak or sing praises to God. Psalm 22:3 says "You dwell where praises are offered." You may feel weakness in your faith, discouraged, or depressed. You may not feel like praising the Lord. That is why it is called "the sacrifice of praise". Hebrews 13:15. When you use praise (even when you don't feel like it), you'll find that praising God brings a sense of God's Presence and Power more quickly than anything else does.

The Power of the name of Jesus Christ of Nazareth is stronger than any other power on Earth because Jesus IS Love and Truth. Smith Wigglesworth says "I know that through His name and through the Power of His name we have access to God….I am here to tell you that there is Power in Jesus and in His wondrous name to transform anyone, to heal anyone." Healing is called "the children's bread" in Mark 7:24-30. We know that all Healing is for the glory of God—to magnify His name and bring others to the truth of His love, forgiveness, and power. A marvelous book that gives clarity to the Biblical reasons we know it is God's will to heal everyone who comes to Him for salvation and who seeks healing to glorify and better serve Christ, is "Christ the Healer" by F.F. Bosworth, (1924).

I encourage you to seek healing by:

1. Seek your salvation in Jesus Christ. God our Father wants to save every person, but he does not force us to believe in Him. He is the ultimate gentleman and gives each one of us the choice….the decision. Romans 10:13 says "Everyone who calls on the name of the Lord shall be saved." If you are not certain that you are saved and you now want to be, Romans 10:8-10 gives the simple steps to becoming a Christian. You can pray the following prayer for salvation:

    "Father God, I believe that in your great love You sent Your Son Jesus Christ to show me how to live, and to die for my sins. You raised Him from the dead and He lives now. I confess that Jesus is my Lord and Savior. Thank You for Your gift of forgiveness and eternal life. Amen."

2. <u>If you know that you are saved</u>, but realize that you haven't been living empowered in the knowledge of all your rights in your Redemption through Christ, you can pray:

"Father God, I thank You for my salvation and redemption in Jesus Christ. Strengthen me through studying what Your Will is in the Word of God, praying, and seeking a deeper relationship with You. Guide me to learn of all my rights as a Christian in this life on earth, to proclaim those rights, and to act on Your Truth. Amen."

3. <u>If you do not attend a local church</u>: Know that God wants us to be in fellowship with other Believers—for support, strength, wisdom, giving, sharing, and brotherly love. And we are to serve the Lord, often through serving others. Pray for the Lord to guide you to the body of believers that is right for you. If you cannot go to a church for health reasons, then perhaps you can seek a small Bible study group that will give you fellowship and prayer partners, or seek fellowship online. "Where two or three are gathered together in My Name, there I am in the midst of them." Matthew 18:20.

4. <u>Seek professional counseling from a Minister trained in counseling, or a Christian counselor</u>. Preferably choose someone who uses some of the incredible new therapies and healing techniques that are discussed in the last chapter in this book. Support Groups specifically for adult females and for adult males who were sexually abused as children can be very helpful. Some churches have Celebrate Recovery groups such as these. 12 step Recovery programs can also help bring about miracles.

To me and many other followers of Christ, the overwhelming realization of the Love of Christ for us, and that He loved us first, fills us with awe and joy. No human is capable of loving you as much as Christ loves you. No person can help you or heal you as much as Christ can. Just ask Him to show you His unconditional life-changing Love. Let yourself fall in love with Jesus Christ, our Lord.

In closing this chapter on "Healing Through Christ" I want to share an incredible poem by Beth Moore, Christian author and teacher.

"DID HE NOTICE ME?"

I was a high school girl in a little bitty world,
Life was 'IF he'd notice me'.
Would my hair do right?
Were my clothes too tight?
What would everybody 'round me think?

I was SO insecure,
Pretending I was pure.
Could they tell that I'd been used?
Friends with all the other girls,
Who came from pretty little worlds,
Would they like me—if they knew?

I was one girl here,
And another girl there,
Seeing which one would survive.
Trying to look like I fit,
All the while wondering—IF
I'd make it out ALIVE?

No place to confess,
My life was a mess.
Had to act like someone else.
Did what others told me to,

While it <u>ripped</u> my soul in two!
Then in the dark all by myself.....
I cried.

Did he notice me?
If he looked what did he see?
Am I worth MORE than I feel?
Will someone fight for me?
Strangle demons til I'm FREE?
Love me long and hard until.....
I'm someone else?

That high school girl in that little bitty world,
Wondering 'If he'd notice me',
Is a long way past.
But the questions that she asked
Found answers gradually.

Turns out.....not many girls come from pretty little worlds.
They ALL needed someone Strong—
That when Truth be told,
And the night turned cold—
Could make Right so much wrong.

A safe place to confess
When life is a mess.
Finding LOVE like no where else.

SOMEONE who <u>had</u> noticed her,
Thought her worth HIS whole world,
And changed how she saw herself.
That same ONE came to fight for me.
Fought my demons,
Set me FREE!

Seems I'm WORTH more than I <u>felt</u>.
HE loved me like I was,
Held me tight,
Taught me Trust,
Til that girl was someone else.
Somewhere ------ <u>HE</u> noticed me.

I now quote one of the most hopeful Scriptures in the Bible, Ephesians 3:14-21

For this reason I kneel before the Father, from whom every family in Heaven and on earth derives its name. I pray that out of His glorious riches He may strengthen you with power though His Spirit in your inner being, so that Christ may dwell in your hearts through faith. And I pray that you, being rooted and established in love, may have power together with all the Lord's Holy people, to grasp how wide and long and high and deep is the love of Christ, and to know this love that surpasses knowledge—that you may be filled to the measure of all the fullness of God.

Now to Him who is able to do immeasurably more than all we ask or imagine, according to His power that is at work in us, to Him be the glory in the church and in Christ Jesus throughout all generations, for ever and ever! Amen.

BIBLIOGRAPY

Biology of Belief, Dr. Bruce Lipton, Mountain of Love/Elite Books, 2005

Biology of Perception, Dr. Bruce Lipton, DVD Spirit 2000

Childhood and Society, Erik Erickson, W.W. Norton Co., Inc. 1950

Christ the Healer, F.F. Bosworth, Chosen Books, 1924

"Did He Notice Me?", Beth Moore, CD of Speeches 2011

EMDR, The Breakthrough Therapy for Overcoming Anxiety, Stress, and Trauma, Dr. Francine Shapiro and Margot Silk Forrest, Basic Books, 1997, 2004, 2016

Ever Increasing Faith, Smith Wigglesworth, Gospel Publishing House, 1924

"Examination of Conscience" 1/2019, Netflix Spanish Docuseries about Infamous Church Child Sexual Abuse Cases.

"Letting Go", Harriet Brown, Oprah Magazine, May, 2011

<u>Passionate Marriage</u>, Dr. David Schnarch, W.W. Norton & Co., 1997

<u>Power vs. Force</u>, Dr. David Hawkins, Hay House, 1995

<u>Praying God's Word- Breaking Free of Spiritual Strongholds</u>, Beth Moore, B & H Publishing Group, 2009

<u>PSYCH-K, The Missing Peace In Your Life</u>, Rob Williams, 1988

<u>Psychology of Change</u>, Rob Williams, DVD Spirit 2000

<u>Satan's Dirty Little Secret</u>, Steve Foss, Creation House, 2007

<u>Sexual Anorexia</u>, Patrick Carnes, Hazelden, 1997

<u>So Long Insecurity</u>, Beth Moore, Tyndale House Publishers, 2010

<u>The Body Keeps the Score</u>, Dr, Bessel Van der Kolk, Penguin Books, 2014

<u>The Course on Weight Loss</u>, Marianne Williamson, Hay House, 2010

<u>The Curves Magazine</u>, Winter 2001

<u>The Divided Mind</u>, Dr. John Sarno, Regan Books, 2006

<u>The Family</u>, Dr. John Bradshaw, Health Communications, Inc., 1988, 1996

<u>The EFT Manual</u>, Gary Craig, Energy Psychology Press, 2010

<u>The Genie in Your Genes</u>, Dr. Dawson Church, Hay House, 2014

"The Keepers", a Netflix Original Documentary Series about child sexual abuse by Catholic priests in a Baltimore high school for years, and an unsolved murder of a nun from the school, 4/2017

The Sexual Healing Journey, Wendy Maltz, William Morrow, 1991, 2001, 2012

The Spontaneous Healing of Belief, Gregg Braden, Hay House, 2008

The Wounded Heart, Dr. Dan Allender, Nav Press, 1990, 2008

Total Money Makeover, Dave Ramsey, Thomas Nelson, 2003, 2007

When A Man You Love Was Abused, Cecil Murphrey, Kregel Publishers, 2010

Who Switched Off My Brain?, Dr. Caroline Leaf, Inprov Ltd., 2008

Win Every Battle, Michael Galiga, Bronze Bow Publishing, 2009

Women, Food, & God, Geneen Roth, Scribner, 2010

You Are the Placebo, Dr. Joe Dispenza, Hay House, 2014

Holy Bible, New King James Version, Thomas Nelson, Inc., 1982, 2006